MEMORIES

HOPE IS THE QUESTION

Memories

Hope is the Question

Dr Richard Bandler & Owen Fitzpatrick

Copyright © 2014 Dr Richard Bandler & Owen Fitzpatrick

The techniques included in this book are based upon the work of Dr Richard Bandler. Such techniques must not be used without express written permission from Dr Bandler.

First published in 2014 by Mysterious Publications.

10 8 6 4 2 1 3 5 7 9

The right of Dr Richard Bandler and Owen Fitzpatrick to be identified as the Authors of the Work has been asserted by them in accordance with the Copyright, Designs and Patents Act, 1988.

All rights reserved. No part of this publication may be reproduced, stored in a retrieval system, or transmitted, in any form or by any means without the prior written permission of the publisher and authors, nor be otherwise circulated in any form of binding or cover other than that in which it is published and without a similar condition being imposed on the subsequent purchaser (including electronic and audio reproductions).

ISBN 978-0-9551353-1-6

Typeset in 12/15 Goudy by Artwerk Limited (artwerk@iol.ie)

Printed and bound in Dublin by Brunswick Press (http://www.brunswickpress.ie)

Mysterious Publications

466 Orwell Park Green, Templeogue, Dublin 6W, Ireland

owen@owenfitzpatrick.com

The last year and a half we lost friends and co-workers that will never be replaced… DR RON PERRY and JEFF SCHOENER.. you both will be missed. Over the years, colleagues we lost such as WILL McDONALD, DAVID NORTHROP, JOHN BROWN (Brownie), ANTON RAPS have all passed into the great beyond. With gratitude and admiration we say goodbye.

Richard:

And from the heart

To my friend Jag who took such good care of me. Always inspiring, always on target.

To Glenda, who showed that fantasies do become real. . .

Owen:

To my parents, Marjorie and Brian Fitzpatrick, for being examples of everything good in life and for giving me all I could ever have wanted.

To my god daughters, Aoife & Lucy, for giving me the greatest reason to be happy.

CONTENTS

INTRODUCTION: Adventures in Real Time 1

SECTION 1: THE INSIDER'S GUIDE TO THE BRAIN 5
1. The Seeds of a Revolution 8
2. The Early Years of NLP 13
3. A Brief History of NLP Patterns 15
   - Anchoring: Triggers of emotion 15
   - Submodalities: The inner qualities of your thoughts 18
   - Representational systems and eye-accessing cues: Clues to how we think 20
   - Strategies: The steps to success 23
   - Hypnosis: The road to your unconscious 24
4. You're Completely Wrong 28
5. Random Ramblings: You're Absolutely Right 32

SECTION 2: BRAINS, LANGUAGE AND COMPUTERS 35
6. Innovations of the Mind 38
   - Design human engineering 39
   - Neuro-hypnotic repatterning 42
7. Software for the Mind: Powerful Techniques for Life Change 46
   - Changing personal history 47
   - Godiva chocolate pattern 49
   - Compulsion threshold pattern 50
8. Pimp your Brain 53
9. Random Ramblings: Snakes and Mistakes 58

SECTION 3: SMARTER EVER AFTER 61
10. Rethinking Happiness 64
    - Propulsion systems 68
11. Decisions on the Future 70
12. The antidote to the Recession 72
13. Mental Security 77
14. Random Ramblings: The Race to Intelligence 80

SECTION 4: MAGICAL LANGUAGE 83
15. Assaulting Linguistics 87
  - Meta-model 88
  - Milton model 88
  - Logical influence 89
16. Loving Words 91
17. The Language of Change 96
18. Paradoxes and Presuppositions 102
19. Random Ramblings: Word-weaving 107

SECTION 5: LOVING RELATIONSHIPS 109
20. The Sound of a Broken Heart 112
21. The Ultimate Relationship 115
22. Children of the Revolution 120
23. Mysteries of the Heart 125
24. Random Ramblings: Tea with my Granny 128

SECTION 6: MEDICINE FOR THE SOUL 131
25. The Wisdom of a Shaman 134
26. Altering Realities 138
27. Healing the Planet 142
28. The Great Influences 144
29. The Angels of Your Life 151
30. The Richest Person Ever to Have Lived 156
31. Memories for Tomorrow 158
32. Random Ramblings: The Most Beautiful Place on Earth 163

CONCLUSION: THE PROMISE OF HOPE 165

ACKNOWLEDGEMENTS 169

GLOSSARY 170

RECOMMENDED READING 173

DVD AND CD PRODUCTS 174

WEBSITES 175

THE SOCIETY OF NEURO-LINGUISTIC PROGRAMMING™ 176

Before freedom and love there comes hope. The idea that things can get better. That all can be okay. The power of hope unlocks for us the chains of despair and suffering. Like a hand guiding the way, it tilts our chin up and it points to something we haven't been looking at. It asks us to see more. When we do so, we give ourselves the chance to live with love and to love to live.

INTRODUCTION

ADVENTURES IN REAL TIME

ONE OF THE GREATEST QUALITIES that human beings have is the capacity for hope – the belief that things can be better. It's what inspires prisoners-of-war to face and triumph over, horrendous adversity. It's what pushes people to cope through grief and heartbreak, illnesses and life-changing tragedies. It's what allows us to keep moving forward, come recession or depression.

Hope is a choice. But hoping is not enough. We must take action. Believing that things will get better is not enough, we must take intelligent action to ensure that they do. This means WE need to be smarter. This book has been created to make you smarter. Smarter in how you operate your brain. Smarter in how you deal with the challenges you face. Smarter in how you relate to your loved ones. Smarter in how you think about life.

You get smarter when you have a new perspective. When you have hope and perspective you're in a very strong position, because from there you can create solutions. You can create opportunities. You can create the kind of future you desire.

So, our plan over the next few pages is to help give you hope and perspective so that you become smart enough to take the right kind of actions to change your life. This book is a journey into our past, with one fundamental goal: sharing the wisdom that comes from our experience. That will give you something absolutely essential: perspective. That's what the change process begins with.

This book gives you a glimpse into our worlds and our lives. It explores Richard's and my thoughts on happiness, the recession, "mid-life crises", relationships, parenting, NLP, shamanism, language. It examines some of the greatest influences on the men we have become and why they have influenced us as they have. It explains the origins of the field of NLP and considers where its many techniques and patterns came from. Our aim is to survey some of the experiences that stand out without diving too deeply in, so that you can gain enough of an understanding to help you learn from our experiences.

This book is divided into six sections. Section 1 is an exploration of the beginnings of NLP and of thoughts on the mind; Section 2 examines the foundation for many NLP techniques; Section 3 explores a new perspective on positivity and on handling the modern world; Section 4 considers language and its magical qualities; Section 5 is an exploration of love, relationships and parenting; and Section 6 concludes with a look at spirituality, altered states and the greatest influences on myself and Richard.

Our conversations and memories ranged from the West Coast of America in the 1960s and 70s to North Korea and India in the 2000s. We discussed some of the most important influences and lessons we've ever learned. We want to tell you what we've learned so that you can save yourself some time! As with every interaction with Richard, you'll find that many of the stories we share are designed to influence you unconsciously as well as consciously, in order that you may find yourself making significant positive changes in your life.

Your life is a collection of moments. It's an adventure. A journey you go on. To enjoy this journey to the fullest, you need to understand how to take control over your mind. The book you are about to read offers you learnings to do just that.

SECTION 1:
THE INSIDER'S GUIDE TO THE BRAIN

The West of Ireland, Wednesday, 30 April 2008

"YOU LOOK BETTER ON THE SCREEN THAN IN REAL LIFE", Richard said to me when the show ended.

I laughed. "Thanks, Richard . . . I think", I replied. I was visiting Richard and his wife, Glenda, in the west of Ireland, where they lived and that night a television show I presented, *Not Enough Hours*, was on RTÉ ONE.

I was very proud that my teacher, mentor and friend, Dr Richard Bandler, got to see me on television using the skills he taught me. I was staying with Richard, as I often did, always finding myself enjoying a complete escape from reality in a house placed perfectly between stony hills, green fields and the Atlantic Ocean.

That's one of many fond memories I have of visiting Richard and it also happens to be the beginning of our story.

In the autumn of 2002, when I was twenty-four, I began to write a book with Richard entitled *Conversations with Richard Bandler*. Richard is regarded by many as being one of the greatest creative geniuses of our era in the field of self-improvement and personal transformation. Having jointly founded the field of neuro-linguistic programming (NLP) in the 1970s, he has continued to update this technology and millions of people around the world have benefited from his contributions to personal and professional development.

Through our conversations, I aimed to discover more about the concept of personal freedom. We talked about change and love and heartbreak and grief and spirituality and stress – and, well, so many different aspects of life.

Writing that book changed me. The book was different from many (NLP) books for three main reasons: it was brutally honest, it was personal and it was from the heart.

The conversations never stopped. I had more questions. Richard had more answers. This time I would explore the beginnings of NLP – questions that had burnt inside me since I first came across it all those years ago. I would enquire about the origins of many of Richard's ideas. I would seek to find the influences that shaped his genius. I would again search, even more deeply, for wisdom on love, life and spirituality.

Furthermore, my own life would take many twists and turns. I would change and be challenged. From all of this, this book would take root and be developed. After the show, Richard and I sat in his kitchen and we began our conversations.

1. THE SEEDS OF A REVOLUTION

I HAVE BEEN DOING NLP FOR MORE THAN TWENTY YEARS, having read my first book on the subject when I was just fourteen years old. That was the beginning of my own personal revolution where everything changed for me.

You see, back then, as a teenager, I hated myself and my life and all I could see was a dark, horrifying, lonely future. I thought far too much, was extremely sensitive and read people easily. It's a very useful skill in the profession I'm in, but back then it was a curse. I could tell who looked down on me, who didn't like me and how I was perceived. The reality was that I felt a loser – a reject, plain and simple.

Where I come from, you made yourself known in the jungle that is your school years by being good at sports or making friends with the cool or good-looking people. I didn't ace it in any of those fields. I was strange. I've always been strange. I never fully fitted in at school, just as I've never really fitted in to normal life. Back then, it was the worst thing in the world. I was bullied. Back then, it got so bad that I wanted to end it all. Suicidal thoughts were ever present.

Nowadays, I have problems of course, but I like myself and my life more than ever. Some would call it a dream life. I get to fly around the world teaching tens of thousands of people how to improve themselves and their lives. I've travelled to eighty countries and taught workshops all over the world, from Bogotá in Colombia to Osaka in Japan. I have studied negotiation at Harvard Business School, presented my own programme on national television and worked with Olympic athletes and billionaires, kids with challenging behaviour, people with suicidal tendencies and CEOs who want to present themselves better on stage or to the media. I've shared the stage with Richard Branson and have worked with multinational companies that want to boost their sales by using the latest, most cutting-edge tools of persuasion, applied psychology and behavioural science. My whole life transformed as a result of what Richard taught me. What is interesting is that NLP itself was born out of a revolution.

In their first book, *The Structure of Magic*, the joint founders of NLP, Dr Richard Bandler and his colleague at the time, John Grinder, referred to *The Structure of Scientific Revolutions* by Thomas S. Kuhn. Kuhn's hugely popular theory posited that scientific theories often undergo a "paradigm shift", whereby a discovery prompts us to think about things in a dramatically different way.

Neuro-linguistic programming came before the popularisation of "coaching", which is now a billion-dollar industry. It came before many in the field of psychology itself began to move away from psychoanalysis and to embrace the importance of changing how we think, rather than examining why we have problems.

In many ways, NLP came to a number of conclusions about human behaviour thirty years before researchers started declaring them. Such audacity requires a special way of thinking. So, my first question was an attempt to find out more about the influences that got Richard thinking as he did back then.

OF: I'd like to start out by asking you about any particular defining memories you have from the time before you began the process of creating NLP – maybe things at the very start, around 1970–71, that kind of era – when you developed certain attitudes that facilitated the discoveries that you had when you first started to create the technology of NLP.

RB: Well, I can go way back before that. I remember having a mechanical clock. And, one day, it stopped working. It was just a little wind-up clock; you wound it up and it had a little alarm on it and hands that went around. It wasn't very expensive, but I didn't have much money and I remember I'd had the clock for a long time. I don't even know where it came from; somebody gave it to me.

When it broke I remember my stepfather telling me, "Just throw the damn thing out." I remember thinking to myself, well, if I'm going to throw it out, what I really ought to do is take it apart and figure out what's inside it. So I remember taking it apart and looking at all the stuff that was inside it. I had no idea. I'd never seen the inside of a clock or anything like it and I couldn't imagine all the pieces that were in there. I remember looking at all these things and there were little gears and springs and all kinds of stuff and thinking to myself that I'd never get this back together.

So, very slowly, I started taking it apart and laying them in order so that I could stop at any point and put things back in the reverse order. And I literally laid it across the floor of a room, piece by piece in a certain order and left the tools in order as well, because I didn't have many – just a screwdriver and a pair of pliers. At a certain point in time there was a little brass spring that, when I went to take it out, was already loose. I remember, as I was trying to take it out, I twisted it and I heard a click. And the minute it clicked, something started rotating and the clock started ticking. So I started putting the stuff back in, wound it up and sat there watching that clock and listening to it tick. Something in my brain went, if you're methodical enough, you could fix anything.

Another time, I took an engine apart and did the same thing. I didn't know much about cars, but I got a car for ten dollars with a blown engine, took it apart piece by piece and laid it on the floor of a garage. When I put it back together it ran. I'm not sure why it didn't run in the first place; it could have been something simple. But by taking it all the way apart and putting it all the way back together, I pretty much covered everything, so that, without spending much money, I ended up with a car that ran. By doing things like that, part of what I learnt was patience and I think for me that's one of the things that's important.

I know it seems, because I do things quickly, that I'm impatient – there is a part of me that wants to get things done quickly, as quick as possible – but I'm very patient in making sure that I look at all the pieces that I could possibly see and notice how they work.

That's done me a lot of good in a lot of areas. I remember the first time I fired a bow and arrow. I was very awkward and it was very hard and I didn't even remotely hit the target. I remember the other people there that had handed me this bow and arrow just laughed at me, because they'd been doing it for a while.

I remember I went out that night and I took the same bow and arrow and I fired it over and over. I did different things. First, I did it really wrong and then tried to figure out what would make it hit what I wanted it to. I mean, I literally took wild shots to try to figure out how to make the mistakes that I was making on purpose, so that I could figure out how to do it better. I didn't have anybody teach me how to do it correctly.

When you tune a guitar, it's very difficult if you try to do it in little turns. Now they have guitar-tuners, but you had to build them in your head in the old days. Having the patience to be able to tune a guitar or to take an engine apart and put it back together, to look at machines and realise that if you engineer things in a certain way when you take them apart and you put them back together, then I reached the point where I started realising that you could modify things, that you could make a car better than what it was.

You could bore out the engine and get more power. You could supercharge it and by getting rid of the carburettor you could actually make it a more efficient device. If you put better tyres on it, it would run better.

Richard seemed to think about the mind in the same way he thought about clocks. But he was even more methodical and efficient in how he thought about it. It was fascinating to hear Richard explain these rare memories of what got him thinking the way he did. Most people seem to enter the personal-enhancement world after going through some significant trauma. They talk about how bad they felt and how they overcame such a challenge and were motivated by it. Indeed, my own experience in being depressed as a teenager was a significant factor in my getting into the field in the first place. Check out the vast majority of gurus and you will find they have the story of struggle in common. Very often it is true, as in my case, but it's one way of reaching out to people who find their circumstances challenging and saying "I was like that too and I changed things."

Richard's entry into it, however, was born out of curiosity about how things worked and how to get things working in the most efficient way possible. Instead of focusing on what he had been through, he explained what he had noticed. It was a radically different approach, but perhaps it explained how he was able to notice and think of things nobody else did. He continued:

RB: When I first encountered the notion of psychotherapy in college, they made us go to a kind of encounter group as part of enrolling in college in my first year. Everybody sat around and whined about their problems and, while it was fun and everything, it didn't really change anybody in any profound way. I don't think anybody really expected it to either. The whole notion was that change was slow and painful. I never even figured out why they made us do it. How was this part of college? I didn't get it. It was like they were trying to employ counsellors and didn't know what to do with them or something.

When I first watched the psychotherapist Virginia Satir I saw her work with a family. A lot of people were there, too, to learn from her. The problem was that everything they said to me presupposed that they weren't going to be able to learn to do what Virginia was doing. It was shocking to me.

I couldn't believe that people had paid all this money to watch this woman do something and then would make a comment like "She's so intuitive." What that translated to was: "I don't have to learn this, because I'm not her." A lot of what she did was linguistically very methodical. There was no reason why anybody could not learn to do what she did; it wasn't that complicated.

I remember talking to her about it. I said, "I don't get it. Why don't they just do what you do?" And Virginia said, "Well, they do try. . ." But I didn't get it. Nobody even looked at the little things she did. I noticed that the way she asked questions was very methodical. She didn't know it consciously, but it was.

I figured out, at that instant, that therapists weren't being methodical about what they were doing with human beings. They were more interested in the theory and the name and it was like psychotherapy had clubs: you were a psychoanalyst; you were a transactional analyst. They all had a little language that they spoke and they taught their patients to speak the language.

But there wasn't any emphasis on getting results. None whatsoever. They were like batches of excuses and the whole thing to me was, they weren't fixing the clock! To me, the big insight was that it was time for somebody to come along and start fixing the clock!

I tried everything. I went to every kind of psychotherapy; I went and watched people do rational emotive therapy, analytical therapy, transactional analysis; I went to Esalen [retreat centre] and let them do all sorts of crazy kinds of treatment on me, like "rolfing". I tried everything under the sun to try and figure out what would work and I ultimately hit the point when modelling psychotherapy taught me that they were engaged in the wrong activity.

First, I wanted to be able to model the best psychotherapists and do it in one approach to change work. That's part of where the "meta-model" came from – taking the best of the questioning techniques therapists used. But what we really discovered was that the meta-model outlined all the things they *could* do, not all the things they *did* do.

Noam Chomsky had done the work with transformational linguistics on figuring out what the form of sentences were. What we figured out how to do was to ask questions based on the form. Chomsky built a model of how language was structured related to our neurology and we built a meta-model, which explained how to use the existing model. I think that looking at structure rather than content was the big deal. Psychotherapists said, "Well, look at the process." But they didn't really look at the process. That's not what they were really doing. They were defending their theories and not their lack of results.

To me, I found the whole thing dissatisfying, because the clock wasn't ticking. That's part of why I started with real basic stuff like phobias, because the proof was in the pudding. The client had either gotten on the escalator or they hadn't. To me, the big insight was that at a certain point in time I realised they were all Freudians, every one of them, even if they disagreed with Freud a hundred per cent. They were doing the same thing he was doing. They had a theory of personality that was more important than the techniques they were using.

What I had always found fascinating about learning from Richard all these years, as a psychologist, was the fact that he thought in a radically different way about the mind and how people think. Instead of assuming that their problems were based on causes and trying to find out what those causes were, Richard examined what the person was doing in relation to their problem and how they could do something differently.

What this means is that, as with a clock or a car, he is always looking for how things work and for a clear and specific understanding of what exactly people do in their heads when they feel bad or stressed or afraid or worried. Once he finds that out, he can help them to do something differently so that they're able to think and feel differently as a habit.

The coolest part is that, for the last forty years, he has been able to share that knowledge with millions of people around the world so that we can know how problems "work" – how to take them apart and put new ways of thinking back together. Understanding Richard's way of thinking led me to explore in more depth the very beginnings of NLP.

2. THE EARLY YEARS OF NLP

THERE ARE HUNDREDS OF BOOKS and thousands of websites where you can find a description of what NLP is and different stories about where it came from. It's described as an attitude, a methodology and a technology; the technology of achievement; the science of success; the study of the structure of subjective experience. Depending on where you read about it, you will learn about different applications for it.

The history of NLP is quite an interesting one. In summary, these are the facts: Richard Bandler met John Grinder at the University of California, Santa Cruz, in the early 1970s. They worked together, studying Fritz Perls, Virginia Satir and Milton Erickson, before going on to study some other highly successful people over the next few years. The form of study they took is known as "modelling" and involves understanding the actual practice of how people think, rather than dwelling on the theories themselves. They would look at what a person does rather than at how they describe what they do.

Modelling is the process of building a conceptual model in order to represent some phenomenon. For example, if you want to be able to build a skyscraper you will first build a working model. This will show you what you need to do to create it. Richard and John built a model of what these successful therapists were doing so that they could get the same results. I wanted to learn more about the early modelling projects.

> OF: When you first started, one of the first people that you modelled was Fritz Perls.
>
> RB: Well, I modelled a lot of his stuff. I had to. I had a lot of films of Fritz. I saw Fritz work. I was hired to work on some of his books. Fritz was like the superstar of the humanistic movement, but he didn't do giant seminars.
>
> Virginia did very big seminars, but Fritz would put thirty people in a room and analyse their dreams and he had a lot of these people that came and studied with him endlessly. He viewed himself as being pitted against Freud. The problem was that basically they all believed there was such a thing as a "personality" and that it was formed from early childhood and that by understanding it you would change.
>
> That was Freud's whole thing. If you understood yourself, then, miraculously, you would change. And whether it comes through Gestalt therapy or whatever, that one thing always was there. By understanding yourself – kapoof! – magically you would rise above it. But that's not really the way it works. You have to have a new way of understanding to understand differently.
>
> OF: So there's obviously a lot of differences between Gestalt therapy and NLP. Is there anything that you found was useful?
>
> RB: Fritz used a few pretty good language patterns and got people to act out things. Whether it was non-verbal behaviours or parts of dreams, or whatever it was, he got people to act instead of just talking about it. Unfortunately, there's a lot he didn't get them to do, because he really didn't believe you could

cure people of any kind of schizophrenia or psychotic behaviour properly. Fritz was still trying to get people to understand what went wrong. And to me that was the whole failing presupposition of psychology. The whole focus was mismanaged.

The best thing about the past is that it's *over*. Understanding how you got screwed up is not going to help you to not be screwed up. It's going to help you screw up other people. That seems to be all it really does. When people ask, "Is there a difference between NLP and Gestalt therapy?", I say there's a difference between NLP and all things that are therapeutic, because NLP is not therapeutic: it's educational. You're teaching people new ways of thinking, to accomplish new things. You get them to process information in a new way and you get a different result. We are all a by-product of how we process information. If we keep processing it the same way, we get the same results.

In my own studies in psychology at university I had a class in Gestalt therapy. I was already well versed in NLP, so I found some similarity in terms of the notion of utilisation. By taking the problems a person had and putting them in such a form that you could do something with them, people had a chance to deal with their problems more easily. For example, by taking a part of you that was critical and imagining the "critical you" sitting in a chair, you could argue with that part of you and it could help you feel better about the critical part.

Of course, there were limits to this approach, as it seemed to continuously emphasise that you needed to finish unfinished business by acting out the issues. The reality, though, is that every event is finished and unfinished, depending on what you decide about it. You don't need to scream at a chair in which you imagine someone who wronged you sitting in order for you to get it "out of your system". There are other options – ones that involve changing in what Richard calls "grown-up and intelligent ways".

As Richard explained, NLP took some ideas from Gestalt therapy. But rather than borrowing its humanistic theoretical underpinnings and delving into Perls's reasoning about what was going on, Richard noticed what Perls seemed to do to help the client feel better about a particular issue and managed to replicate it.

The difference between NLP and most other approaches is that it's focused on what you need to do differently rather than on looking for "why" you have a problem. So, whatever problems you have in your life right now, we would aim to find out how you think about it rather than where it came from. That's the secret sauce.

3. A BRIEF HISTORY OF NLP PATTERNS

SOON AFTER MODELLING PEOPLE LIKE PERLS, Satir and Erickson, a number of patterns and techniques were created that became the foundation of NLP. A new technology was born that allowed you to work with someone with a phobia and help them overcome it in a very short space of time and to do many other things besides. Terms such as "representational systems", "anchoring", "eye-accessing cues", "strategies" and "submodalities" were used to explain certain parts of the new NLP model. I wanted to ask Richard about the origins of these patterns.

Anchoring: Triggers of emotion
For me, one of the best aspects of the field of NLP is the idea that we can associate an internal feeling with a behaviour and not just rely always on purely observable phenomena. This is known as "anchoring". The concept of "behaviourism" has helped us understand that we make associations between good behaviour and reward and between bad behaviour and punishment. But actually exploring the idea that individual subjective feelings have triggers or behavioural cues was new. For me, anchoring is still one of the most important parts of NLP.

If, for example, you make a move or gesture when you're feeling excited, that gesture or movement will allow you to trigger the feeling when you want it back ("stimulus-response conditioning").

The consequences of this are exciting to ponder. If you have a presentation coming up that you want to be more confident for, all you have to do is create that feeling by imagining how you would look, sound and feel at your most confident. Then, once you're feeling extremely confident, the next step is to find some trigger for yourself, such as pressing together your thumb and index finger while you're experiencing that feeling. When you do this you will associate the feeling with that trigger and when you're about to stand up and speak you'll just need to press together your index finger and thumb and the feeling will return. Of course, the more you practise this the more you will master it.

> OF: Richard, I wanted to talk to you about your memories of when you first discovered anchoring – when you first realised that anchoring was something that was useful.
>
> RB: It was actually kind of an odd thing, to tell you the truth. Somebody was talking about what they were angry about and I reached over and interrupted them by just touching them on the leg and I reminded them of something that they'd just talked about earlier which they were really happy about and they started being really happy. And after a couple of minutes – I don't know what possessed me – I leaned forward and just touched them on the knee and they suddenly got angry. They didn't get angry at me: they got angry about the same thing they'd been angry about before. I remember reading in *Body and Mature Behaviour* [by Moshé Feldenkrais] about something similar – about "stimulus-response conditioning" and of course the name Pavlov rang a bell immediately.

Ivan Pavlov was a psychologist regarded as a pioneer in the area of "classical conditioning" in behaviourism, a branch of psychology. Pavlov conducted an experiment whereby he fed dogs at the same time as sounding a bell. He did this a number of times; later he would sound the bell without food and the dogs salivated. This resulted in the theory that we associate a stimulus (the sound of the bell) with a response (the salivation in anticipation of food). So the stimulus leads to the response.

> RB: I thought to myself, wouldn't it be bizarre if it was that simple? one-trial learning, as in, you learn from doing the experience once, as opposed to building a stimulus-response conditioning with M&M sweets over a long period of time, like they were trying to do in elementary schools at the time. I just started to experiment.
>
> I remember when we first started doing anchoring I even had my students take lessons from mime artists, because mime artists can be so precise with their movements that they create visual images. It wasn't that I wanted my students to be mime artists, but I wanted them to realise that the way in which they moved every part of their body had to be precise, so that they created a precise signal.
>
> Anchoring isn't something I think a lot about now, because it's become second nature to me. The fact that people talked about stimulus-response conditioning for so long and all the studies with Pavlov and all that stuff and they never really sorted out the difference between human beings and dogs. Dogs are just a lot more intelligent about things in certain ways, but human beings are capable of learning a lot faster.
>
> Humans can do one-trial learning. They don't do it a lot, because the signals need to be really, really precise. The interesting thing about Pavlov's work wasn't so much that the dog would salivate when they'd fire the 440 tone; it was that, as they changed the tone to 345 or 330 – as they moved away from 440 to 435 or 420 – the amount of salivation decreased proportionately. Then the really interesting thing, which even the researchers didn't understand and didn't talk about, was that if they stopped providing the steak that made the dog salivate, then when they'd ring the bell the dog would begin to snap at the researcher. When the stimulus failed to produce the response, then the dog would get angry again because it had been cheated out of its steak.
>
> That's the difference between human beings and dogs: after a while the dog will stop responding to the cue if there's no steak. Human beings, on the other hand, I believe, will do it for ever. That's the power of our ability to have ideas. This is why, when people start taking some kind of drug, it has a really powerful positive effect at first and then they build up a tolerance to it. They don't even get anything good from it, but they're addicted to it. Their brain still thinks that when they take this it's going to make them feel better, even if it doesn't.
>
> I've talked to crack addicts and cocaine addicts and freebasers who know they're not getting high, but it's just stopping them from feeling bad. I go, "Why don't you just go through withdrawal and get it over with? Every day you get up and you're shaking; you should be going one day closer to being free of this."

And they go, "Yeah, but when I think about doing it, I just know it's going to give me a rush."

I go, "Really? But you said it didn't."

They go, "Well, it might."

Human beings have this notion of thinking their way through responses. To me, the immediacy with which you can get a human being to trade or change their feelings is the importance of anchoring. By anchoring you can get a really powerful response.

I do it mostly tonally now. I talk with them about something in one tone of voice and then keep my tone of voice the same and talk about things that are difficult and my tone of voice doesn't reflect it. It reflects either humour or something else and people will start laughing at things that they couldn't discuss without crying ten minutes earlier. Our ability to change how we feel about things and all the techniques that NLP offers to do that, are in part a reflection of initially discovering anchoring close to four decades ago.

The process of anchoring is particularly useful for two reasons. One is that it enables you to feel the way you want to feel when you want to. For example, one of the most practised techniques is what we call "brilliance squared". In it, we have a person imagine a square in front of them on the ground with an image of them standing in it as they would stand at their most confident. We get them to vividly imagine it all and then to step into the square. When they step in they find themselves in the same posture as that self in the square. With a little practice, this allows them to feel instantly confident when they need to, simply by imagining the square and stepping into it. In this case, the act of stepping into the square becomes the anchor and when they do it in the future we refer to that as "firing off" the anchor.

So, anchoring becomes useful because you get to change your state quite powerfully by creating a positive feeling and firing it off when you need it. Even if something has been making you feel bad, you can fire off a positive feeling at the same time as you experience whatever has made you feel bad and by doing so you'll cancel the impact of the negative feeling. For example, if you think about someone and feel intimidated, you can create a really positive feeling of strength and assertiveness and anchor it. Then, when you think about the person, fire off the feeling of assertiveness and you'll feel significantly better about them. This becomes unconscious over time.

The second way in which anchoring is particularly useful is in how you can use it with other people. You can influence other people more effectively by creating positive feelings and associating them with what you want the person to feel good about. Or you can create negative feelings and associate them with what you want the person to feel bad about. For example, you can create a good state in the other person and then associate it with your product. Then you can create a negative state in the other person and associate it with a competitor's product. How would this work?

Imagine, for example, that I wanted to create a positive feeling in you and link it to the iPhone and also to create a negative feeling in you and link it to the BlackBerry phone. Here's what I might do: I'd talk to you about good decisions you'd made that you were really happy with. I'd talk about investments you'd made that were terrific decisions. I'd be extremely positive, all the while gesturing to my right and speaking in a rational, positive and upbeat tone of voice, with a smile on my face.

Then I might talk to you about negative experiences you've had in buying products you wasted money on. I might talk about poor decisions and bad investments you'd made, all the while gesturing to my left and speaking in a slightly negative and whiney tone of voice, with a slight squint.

Then I'd talk to you about the iPhone while gesturing to my right and using a positive, upbeat tone of voice and a smile; and I might mention the BlackBerry while gesturing to my left while using a whiney tone of voice and squinting. This would allow me to associate in your mind positive feelings with the iPhone and negative feelings with the BlackBerry. It's incredibly powerful!

In creating feelings it's not just about mentioning a person's experiences. The way a person thinks about positive and negative thoughts actually determines how powerful these feelings really are. To explore *how* this happens we need to look at submodalities.

Submodalities: The inner qualities of your thoughts
There are a number of important elements in creating a positive and powerful state in the first place. Submodalities are the qualities of the internal images and sounds you create in your mind. For example, when you think a thought it will usually be either in the form of an image or of self-talk. In NLP we examine the actual qualities of that image or self-talk. Whether the image is big or small, focused or blurry, in colour or black and white, those would be examples of the submodalities of your images. The loudness and the tone of your voice are a couple of examples of the submodalities of your inner voice.

> OF: And, close to three decades ago, you discovered the notion of submodalities and how useful that was. Have you any memories to do with that?
>
> RB: Well, we knew that there were synaesthesia patterns originally and it wasn't until the mid-1980s that we got the significance of submodalities. We did use them without realising it. There were anchoring techniques that did things. We did things with phobias where we had people disassociate, but we didn't think about it that way. We weren't capable of doing all the important elicitation that we were able to do later on.
>
> We really sorted that out in the 1980s and discovered the importance, I think. What struck me more than anything was when somebody was trying to get somebody to quit smoking in a seminar. I wasn't even teaching the seminar; I just happened to be walking through the room. The person was arguing with them because they didn't actually want to quit smoking: they wanted to only smoke (I think it was) eleven cigarettes a day, instead of a pack.
>
> I remember thinking, how dumb is that! Either do it or don't do it. I said something to them from the back of the room and the person didn't realise who said it and they turned around and bit my head off. While they were yelling, everybody else in the room knew that it was me. Then something inside their head went, uh-oh! As they were turning around they even said to the person, "That's Richard back there, isn't it?"
>
> When their eyes hit mine you could see their faces change. And when I walked towards them I literally said, "What makes you believe you could smoke eleven cigarettes instead of two packets a day?" I said, "What makes you think that that's a possibility?"

This person literally took their hands and measured things out in the air and said, "When I think about things over here, it seems impossible. Being a person who never smokes a cigarette is in the area of impossibility." Then they moved their hands completely to the other side of their body and they said, "Well, these are the things I think I can do. I think I could get by on eleven cigarettes. But I can never do any of the things that are over here."

I remember looking at the two locations and thinking, why can't we swap those? It's very hard to move a picture straight across your midline and get it to stay there. I don't know why. So I literally took one picture and set it up, took another picture and shrunk one down and made the other one bigger. Thus was born the "swish" pattern. Doing this three times made it so this person never smoked again. It just set my mind: we've got to look at this mathematically.

Now, also at the time, I was running a holographic lab where all we did was work with non-linear variables – distance, intensity of light, polarisation of light. And if you're even a smidgen off on a hologram you get nothing.

Looking at those sixty-four non-linear variables and then looking at submodalities as non-linear variables and coming up with the equations of what made things permanent versus the things that didn't – this was a big math project. While most people in the seminars only saw the results, they didn't realise the amount of pure calculus that was behind this.

When we looked at all the things that we thought of as synaesthesia patterns and looked at the techniques that we had been doing that produced permanent changes and reanalysed everything and built a mathematics for submodalities, it allowed us to compute what else might be there. The birth of a whole horde of new techniques came falling out of the sky and most people didn't understand where it came from.

It came from being able to understand a mathematical model. When you model something it doesn't mean you imitate it: it means you build a calculus for it. That calculus allows you to compute what else is out there that will do similar things, or different things. With enough experience in years gone by, we may have stumbled on these techniques. But being able to compute them quickly took the field of NLP and took its technology and sent it through the ceiling. It allowed us to do a thousand times more things than what we were able to do the year before. And, to me, that's what made submodalities such an important step in NLP.

Representational systems and eye-accessing cues: Clues to how we think
Before submodalities came along, there had already been the discovery of eye-accessing cues. These suggest that when a person moves their eyes in a particular direction they are either making images, talking to themselves, hearing internal sounds, or processing feelings. When you ask a person a question, in order for them to answer they will have to retrieve the information from their mind. To do this most people tend to move their eyes in a particular direction. By paying attention to this, you can get a good understanding of how exactly they're accessing that information.

For example, if a person's eyes are pointing down to their left it suggests that they're talking to themselves. If they're doing that it's less likely that they will be paying full attention to you. Sometimes their eyes might look down to the right, which suggests that they could be stuck in their feelings.

A few years ago, when Brian Colbert (my friend and business partner from the Irish Institute of NLP) and I were teaching an NLP practitioner in Edinburgh, a woman came up to me at the end of one of the days and told me that she couldn't imagine her future. She had been to therapists and even to a few NLPers and the various techniques they tried on her hadn't worked. To understand what she was talking about, I asked her to think about her future.

Instinctively, her eyes went down to her right and she looked back up at me and said, "I can't."

On seeing this, I said, "Okay, I want you to look up to your right and keep your eyes looking up there. Now, in doing so, I want you to imagine your future."

As she did this, the expression on her face changed; her eyes lit up as if she was seeing something for the very first time. Everyone else had been trying to do something advanced. I simply noticed that she seemed stuck in her feelings and when I got her out of them it changed what she could do.

These eye-accessing cues are connected to representational systems. This indicates that, by listening to the words a person uses, you can tell how they're processing information as well. The idea suggests that people use visual words such as *see, view, perspective, vision, show* and *look* when they're processing ideas visually; auditory words such as *hear, say, talk, discuss, resonate* and *chat* when they're processing ideas aurally; and kinaesthetic or "feeling" words such as *touch, feel, sit, grab, grip, settle* and *sense* when they're processing ideas kinaesthetically. If you match the sensory words a person uses, you create a better sense of rapport with them, so that the other person is more likely to feel that you understand them.

I had heard Richard give the example of Virginia Satir working with couples who often mismatched each other's representational systems. This turned out to be one of the things that caused conflict between them. Often the woman in the relationship would say that her partner never told her that he loved her, while the man would defend himself by arguing that he did show her that he loved her. Although Satir picked this up unconsciously, it wasn't until Richard and John modelled her that the process was seen to be important.

OF: Representational systems and accessing cues – could you tell us a little about your earliest memories of your experiences with these?

RB: Well, accessing cues were there all along. I read an article in this neurological journal in which they were studying perception and how the eyeballs move when you're looking at something. They found that when they asked people to recall an image of a white house that they showed them, the person's eyes usually shifted up to the left and the researcher said this must mean something.

When I read it I started thinking about it, so I went into a class I was teaching with about three hundred students in it and I just asked them questions. As I did, their eyes all moved in the same direction, except for the people who had their watch on the opposite wrist.

Then we literally made a form and asked people all sorts of questions to notice the response. I'd ask them, "What are the first four notes of Beethoven's symphony?" I had them make a picture of a giraffe with a rhinoceros's head – things that would require them to construct images. I asked them to think about sounds and feelings. I made a big list and sent thirty people out to answer these questions. They did it with partners. They came back and you could just see that there was a pattern to where people's eyes moved.

Really, though, you could see accessing cues in Betty Boop commercials and cartoons from the 1920s and 30s. Everybody's kind of known about it and people responded to it as if it was there. Psychology got this notion that if you looked away, somehow or other you were being insincere. They placed this high value on eye contact. So if you were in therapy and they asked you a question and you looked away, they would go, "What are you avoiding?" That's just nonsense. You were thinking, not avoiding.

For a lot of the questions they asked, the only way you could answer was by accessing the information. Somebody goes, "What do you remember about your mother?" If you look away to get a memory and the psychologist interrupts you and goes, "You're avoiding something", you'll never get to the memory! That's because you're repressing it.

The great thing about accessing cues is that I could take rooms full of psychologists, get them to face each other and have them ask each other questions and predict what would happen. I would have them sit down and I would go, "Ask your partner what colour their mother's eyes are and notice which way their eyes move." And then I'd tell them, "Your eyes went up and to the left", "Your eyes went up to the left", "Your eyes went up and to the right." And their partners would all go, "Yeah, how did you know that?" like it was some big miracle. But it was the first thing that psychologists learnt to see, without interpreting what it meant. It didn't mean that you were a visual: it meant that you were visualising. If I asked you a different question it meant you were remembering auditorially. And if you touched yourself in the mid line and looked down and to the right you'd be accessing feelings.

Then there was representational systems. In the conclusion of his first book, which he wrote before he met me – on Chomsky's transformational grammar – Grinder talked about a much more specific relationship between language and the sensory systems. It's one of those things whose time was there.

You could hear it in the predicates or words a person used. People would look one way and they'd use visual predicates. And they'd look the other way and they'd use auditory predicates. They'd go, "I'm telling myself this. I see it this way. But I feel blah, blah, blah, blah. . ." This allowed us to sort out a lot of what went on in therapy. What they call top dogs and underdogs, subconscious and unconscious – different parts of people. All the metaphorical stuff that psychologists use started out by rep. systems. It allowed psychologists to make a little sense out of what they were doing.

I considered the work on Freud that I had studied. His theories ranged from the interesting to the ridiculous. I remember reading some of his books and finding myself understanding why so many people believed in what he was saying. He could be very persuasive in his writings. But at the end of the day, when you look at it with a more rational mind, you realise that it's all just a metaphorical way of thinking about people's problems. Representational systems differed from what many people were doing because, instead of assuming that we understand what a person means from what they say, we're interested in noticing the very words they use and what that might tell us about them.

One of the key distinctions between NLP and many other approaches to human communication is that you tend to watch and listen to a person more literally. There are a number of misconceptions about eye-accessing cues, for example. In Hollywood movies and in a number of popular books there is a suggestion that when we look up and to the left we're telling the truth and that when we look up and to the right we're lying. This is a misinterpretation of what we actually know. The problem emerges when people feel the need to make assumptions about what they notice.

I remember many years ago talking to a master practitioner at a course on language I was attending. I asked him how it was going. He proceeded to tell me that it was "a bit auditory" for him, as he was a "visual". This is where people get silly. The reality is that there's no such thing as a "visual", an "auditory" or a "kino". These are just patterns that indicate what a person is doing at that particular moment. It does not in any way define a person's "personality". Human beings seem to limit themselves by the labels they give themselves. Labelling yourself often creates a limitation in your mind about what's possible for you.

I then asked the master practitioner what he wanted the trainer to do, speak in sign language? The trainer was teaching us about language. The reality is that people will tell you a lot about how they think if you pay attention, but as soon as you close your mind and assume that they are a "particular kind of person" you miss so much information.

I believe that one of the biggest mistakes that has been made in psychology is in relation to its labelling of psychological illnesses. People are referred to as "depressives", "phobics" and "obsessive-compulsives". Labelling people for the purposes of explaining an idea is one thing; the problem arises when such labels serve to limit someone's belief in their capacity for change. As long as we use such labels for ourselves we will be locked inside a particular idea of who we are. So to avoid making the mistakes that have been made in other areas of psychology, it's important to remember that NLP is largely about paying attention to patterns and what they suggest, rather than using our findings as conclusive evidence about a person's supposedly limited nature.

It's also where one of the fundamental presuppositions or principles of NLP comes in. There is a principle that suggests: "People aren't broken; it's just that the value of their behaviour in a given context can be questioned." So it's not that we're messed up but that we think in messed-up ways, create messed-up feelings and do messed-up things. The question we really need to ask is, "how do we think, feel or act in such messed-up ways?" The answer to this lies in the concept of strategies.

Strategies: The steps to success
Every feeling you have arises either from associations you have with past experiences or from engaging in a process inside your mind that creates that feeling. These processes are called "strategies". If you have a phobia, for example, in order to be afraid of something you have to go inside your mind and make a movie, hear sounds and talk to yourself in such a way that you create that feeling of fear. Different people can look at spiders in very different ways. Someone with a phobia about spiders might delve inside their head and imagine one scurrying about seeming big and frightening; another person might just see it as a small creature minding its own business. At the same time, others who are obsessed with spiders might find themselves in awe of these incredible creatures and all the fascinating aspects of their arachnid lives.

These ways of thinking all occur in the strategies a person uses in their mind. Someone who's nervous about public speaking might imagine themselves in a packed room and picture the audience going quiet and staring at them with big heads and big eyes. They might imagine themselves getting stuck and forgetting what they were about to say and then seeing the audience shaking their heads furiously. If they do this inside their mind, they will create an overwhelming feeling of fear.

On the other hand, if they learn to alter this way of thinking and imagine themselves walking confidently on stage, it changes things. They can imagine themselves speaking naturally with composure and can picture the audience listening with rapt attention, smiling away. They can imagine that, even if they forget what they were supposed to say, they will calmly adjust and take some time to compose themselves before continuing to speak clearly and powerfully. When they think of it in this new way, using this new strategy, they will feel differently. Indeed, many NLP techniques involve helping people to disable a bad strategy that creates a negative feeling and to replace it with a good strategy that creates a positive feeling. I wanted to get Richard's recollections on strategies.

> OF: Where did strategies fit in?
> RB: Well, it was important to sort out the difference in NLP between accessing systems, representational systems and systems that are about convincing yourself, which are different. Then we started looking at the sequence of internal representation systems to see what they did.
>
> Take the strategy of spelling: good spellers make pictures of words that are visually remembered, but they check it with their feelings to make sure they're right. People who have a good memory for names look at a person's face and they make a visually constructed image from it – of a cartoon, or some kind of an exaggeration. Then they hear the name and they see the name. You have systems that have not just one way of checking but a series of ways of checking.
>
> That's when it became obvious that, of the programmes that people use to think, some are better for certain things than for others. You can change that programme, which was the big thing. You could take a bad speller and make him into a good speller. You can take somebody who has trouble making decisions, give them a better decision strategy and they'll make better decisions.
>
> The same thing is true about motivation strategies. There are strategies for all kinds of things. There are strategies that are good for learning to play the guitar; there are strategies that are good for learning to be a good close-up magician. They're not the same. When you have ideas like creativity and talk about it as if it's a "thing", then you're not examining the process. And if you don't examine the process, you can't teach somebody else the process.

One of my favourite examples of the use of strategies in helping someone overcome their problems was reported in Richard's book *Magic in Action*, which is a transcript of videos that show him working with a number of people. Richard worked with a woman who had a problem with anticipatory loss. She was really anxious when people turned up late. He asked her a magical question: "Imagine I was from the temporary problem agency and I had to take over from you for a day. What would I need to do in order to have that problem?"

This allowed her to describe exactly what her strategy was for getting anxious and in this way Richard was able to help her work with it and change it. Helping people in therapy and coaching involves doing what you can to understand what a person is doing, so you can help them to stop doing it and to do something different.

Another way to help people do this is something else Richard used a lot: hypnosis.

Hypnosis: The road to your unconscious

Hypnosis is an altered state in which a person becomes more suggestible. In many ways it's an application of NLP and you can use it as one of the tools that help people change. The model that's often used to explain hypnosis is that we have a conscious mind and an unconscious mind. The conscious mind is the part of our mind that analyses and criticises and thinks logically. The unconscious part is the seat of our imagination and creativity and the source of our memories, wisdom and dreams. It's also where our habits reside. So when you learn something, you might be conscious of the process at first. But after you do it a number of times it becomes automatic and you no longer need to think about it, because you do it unconsciously. For example, you might need to concentrate on many different skills and behaviours when learning to drive, but with enough practice you get to a place where you can automatically drive without even thinking.

The problem is that many of our behaviours or habits of thinking or feeling aren't necessarily good for us. Hypnosis works by creating a state whereby you bypass the conscious mind and are communicating with the unconscious mind, so you can help someone change unconscious processes they might engage in that aren't necessarily useful.

Since I regard Richard as the best hypnotist I have ever seen, I was interested in where his interest in hypnosis began.

> OF: Can you talk to us about the earliest memories you have of learning about the importance and power of hypnosis.
>
> RB: When Gregory [Bateson] told us about Milton Erickson and told us that John [Grinder] and I should go and meet him, Grinder said to me, "Oh, I've always wanted to learn hypnosis." I went out and bought fifty books on hypnosis – a few new ones but mostly really old ones from used-book stores and some that Gregory gave me to read.
>
> I sat down and read about fifty books and went next-door and hypnotised my neighbour. The first thing I realised is that I'd been doing it for years. I got rid of somebody's allergies just by making up something as I went along: someone had terrible hay fever and was living in the middle of a field with everything they're allergic to and their eyes are watering and itching and she can't speak except through her nose. And forty-five minutes later she's outside walking around without any problem.
>
> It struck me that the only hypnosis that I knew about was stage hypnosis. So I took a real serious look at this for anything that could have an immediate impact. Most of the hypnotists were virtually despised by psychotherapists and the fact that psychotherapists were so upset that I was interested in hypnosis interested me. They were almost phobic of hypnosis. They would always tell

me, "Hypnosis doesn't exist and it's bad", which is kind of contradictory, if you think about it. And then they say,

"It only treats the symptom." That seemed like a good thing to me.

They'd say,

"If you suppress the symptom it comes out somewhere else." Now, if you tell a mathematician,

"You scrunch these numbers and they change over here", that's an equation and just didn't sound like a bad thing. Then they would say,

"It's manipulative" and I'd go, "Yeah", because if you say it with bad tonality, manipulative sounds bad. But if you go,

"I'm going to manipulate the position of beads on a table so that it makes a design", nobody gets upset. It was just *mishegas* – nonsense.

These people had just been trained that hypnosis was bad and they never tried it or looked at it. Now, most hypnotists were on the opposing side. They had all of these crazy beliefs about how you were supposed to do stuff and you weren't supposed to go into trance and the other person was and that some people could be hypnotised and some couldn't. It was just all this nonsense and they had research facilities proving what they already thought was the case.

So I just learnt the skills and ignored all the *mishegas*. That's why I became a very good hypnotist. I didn't adopt their limiting beliefs. I just adapted their skill. And that's an important thing to remember: you don't have to take the beliefs to learn the skills.

Hypnosis is something I've been doing for more than twenty years. I read my first book on the subject when I was thirteen or fourteen and, like Richard, immediately started practising on people. I remember starting out doing stage-hypnosis shows at birthday parties when I was still in school, in the very early 1990s, with no formal training. Having become interested after watching a young Paul McKenna on his hugely popular programme *The Hypnotic World of Paul McKenna*, I bought his book of the same name for Christmas and devoured every page. I read it multiple times and saved up any money I could to buy more books on the topic.

Half the time I didn't really know what I was doing, but I was determined to get as good at it as possible, so I kept practising over and over again. I listened to every hypnosis audiotape and videotape I could get my hands on. At one particular party, when I was fourteen, I remember hypnotising about twelve kids – they were all about the same age as me – in a show. I did it in the back room of a big house in my area with the mother and father of the birthday child looking on, alongside the parish priest. You could tell they were nervous.

After a couple of routines working out well and with the thirty or so children at the party laughing, I'd given the volunteers a suggestion that, whenever a phone rang, they would think that the foot of the person next to them was the phone and to try and pick it up. I'd seen Paul do it on his show. Now, I'd planned to ensure that they were in safe positions before this was to happen, but while they were in the middle of another routine the actual phone in the house rang. Chaos ensued and I remember seeing all these legs going flying and people diving on each other and thinking, oh no!

I interrupted the routine, had them relax and got them back into their chairs. After a minute or so of my giving them relaxing suggestions, one person opened his eyes and said he

Richard on stage with hypnotist Paul McKenna

had a headache. My adrenalin started pumping. I had no idea what to do. I saw from the corner of my eye the parents and the priest starting to get anxious. Immediately, I told the boy with the headache that he was going to be okay and that I would work with him. But the show fell apart as, one by one, everyone started opening their eyes and talking about the headache they had.

I don't know what possessed me, but intuitively I smiled and told them all that it was going to be okay and that I would sort them all out immediately. I took them out one by one into the back garden, away from prying eyes and had them stand in front of me. The night was black and I stood with my back to the kitchen. Very light rain clouded their view. With each person, I told them to close their eyes. I then put my hand on their head and said in a fairly dramatic voice, "In a moment I'm going to count from ten down to one . . . By the time I reach one, your headache will not only be gone, but you will feel really wonderful. Ten . . . nine . . . eight . . ." With each person I said the same thing. To everyone's surprise, all twelve volunteers were "cured" and found themselves feeling really good. They were fascinated. The priest didn't need to do any exorcisms, thank God!

I remember that during this experience I was thinking to myself, oh, my God, what's going on? What do I do? However, on the outside I looked confident and powerful and fully in control. That was where I first learnt the importance of belief and the power of suggestion.

Since then I've hypnotised more than ten thousand people in all kinds of contexts, for all kinds of problems. To me, the combination of encouraging someone to take conscious control over their life and the use of hypnosis to help them reprogramme their mind in a more efficient way is extremely effective in helping to create long-term change.

But the memory of one of my earliest experiences with hypnosis never left me. My certainty was my greatest strength. My beliefs were really important. I was convinced of that. However, I soon learnt that they were also my biggest weakness.

4. YOU'RE COMPLETELY WRONG

IN THE AUTUMN OF 2011 I stepped off a plane in Pyongyang. I had wanted to visit for many years. Cut off from the rest of the world, North Korea – or the Democratic People's Republic of Korea (DPRK) to give it its proper name – has always fascinated me. Except for the occasional diplomat, North Koreans were not allowed to leave the country, so it would be very surprising to ever come across one. I was informed that it was a nation of brainwashing and propaganda – a dangerous nuclear power that didn't care at all about the welfare of its people. Ruled by dictator after dictator from the same family, known as the "Dear Leader" and "Great Leader", it seemed untouched by the collapse of communism around the world.

I had heard stories about citizens who were tortured and killed for tearing up a newspaper (all of which have an image of the Dear Leader on them). I had heard about the labour camps and defector stories, with families being separated, never to see each other again – husbands and wives, mothers and sons, brothers and sisters.

I knew the story of the war. After the Second World War the Japanese relinquished control of Korea. North Korea was occupied by the Soviets, while South Korea was occupied by forces from the United States. The "puppet government" in the North then attacked the "democratically elected government" in the South and the Korean War began. After three years and more than two million deaths, mostly civilian, a truce was made. The war never officially ended, but now a strip of land known as the DMZ (Demilitarised Zone) line divides the North and South Korean states. It is positioned at the heart of the country. Below it are the "brave soldiers" of the Republic of Korea. Above it are the "brainwashed terrorist minions" of the DPRK.

After finishing a workshop in Japan, I made my way across to Beijing and from there I took a flight to Pyongyang. I arrived mid-morning. As soon as I stepped off the plane I looked around me. There was fog everywhere. Although it was reasonably warm, the sky was covered by clouds and I got a really eerie feeling. As I went through immigration I half expected to be carted off to a concentration camp for looking at the security officer strangely. But I made it through without a hitch and then went looking for my name on a sign. The image I had of my guides was one of two old men, each a cross between a robot and a grumpy, angry Korean police officer. Then I saw my name. I saw my guides. But they were not old and they were not men.

The two young women who picked me up were dressed neatly and stylishly. One of them had a big smile on her face. The other woman looked neither happy nor sad: she just seemed to carry off neutral. After welcoming me they got into the car with me. They didn't speak much. A million questions passed through my mind. How brainwashed were they? Would they spy on me? Were they being watched? I felt like a character in a spy novel.

Eventually we started small talk. Cho Hee was in her early thirties. She was pretty and wore horn-rimmed glasses. Though she did most of the talking, she wasn't the guide in charge: the other woman was. Also pretty and in her mid-twenties, Hy was as stoic a person as I'd ever met. She didn't smile, but she didn't get depressed either. She just seemed to be somewhere in between – cool as you like. Nothing seemed to ruffle her. As she began explaining some of what was on the agenda, I interrupted her to compliment her on her English. I asked her where she learnt it.

Without skipping a beat, she responded, "I learnt it while studying in the UK."

Completely confused, I stumbled. "Really?" I asked, stunned.

"No", she replied with perfect timing and a dead-pan delivery, "I was joking." I burst out laughing.

People from the Democratic People's Republic of Korea weren't supposed to have a sense of humour, I thought to myself.

Over the next few days I got to know the two women and the driver, Jin, better and better. We played table tennis together. (Never play table-tennis with Korean women. They will embarrass you with their skill.) We talked over drinks. Although they were stand-offish at first, I got to know them better as we talked about all sorts of issues. I was surprised, impressed, taken aback. Here were two intelligent women who had beliefs very different from mine but who weren't insane cult members or broken-down personalities. I just didn't get it.

The tours involved much of the propaganda I had been prepared for, except that some of it seemed to resemble my own education in style. It was confusing. I knew the truth. Yet the Koreans I met believed something else. My confusion grew because, as I started to observe the thought-control policies used by their government, I recognised versions of them in my own country. Movies portrayed the DPRK government as heroic and positioned the Americans as evil, just as for years during the Cold War, American movies positioned the Americans as liberators and the Soviets as evil communists.

I was brought through the DPRK's view of the Korean War. It suggests that in 1950 the "evil American imperialist bastards" invaded the north of Korea and thus began the bloody war. The South Korean "puppet government", together with their "American handlers", forced "innocent Koreans" from the south to fight their northern brethren, against their wishes. The great DPRK army, under the leadership of the great leader Kim Il Sung, forced the South Koreans out and managed to achieve a wonderful victory, which they marked with the truce in 1953. The DPRK labels the Korean War as the "Fatherland-Liberation War." The People's Republic of China officially calls it the "War to Resist US Aggression and Aid Korea".

Looking elsewhere, to the Gulf War, the invasion of Afghanistan, the invasion of Iraq – all are given as examples of America "liberating" these suffering countries. Except . . . not to everyone. When I was in Tibet, a country occupied by China since the 1950s, I went to a museum where I read about how Tibet was liberated *into* the motherland of China. But to some Tibetans it was occupied. Even in the American political system and, in fact, the Irish political system, there are two sides to most issues.

The case of my own country, Ireland, involved a number of big decisions that affected the country significantly. The Anglo-Irish Treaty, signed back in 1921, established the Irish Free State, offering the Six Counties the opportunity to opt out and remain under British rule. Although this ended one war, it led to another. The Treaty brought to an end the War of Independence, but once it had been announced two stances arose in Ireland: those who supported the Treaty and those who opposed it. This disagreement soon culminated in the Civil War, in which, in several cases, families were split for and against the Treaty. Even with the same upbringing and culture there is still room for two completely different interpretations of events and two very different beliefs about right and wrong!

My point here isn't political. It's not designed to provoke controversy or defend the communist-governed countries or dictatorships and their way of ruling. Indeed, much of it I'm strongly against. What I'm talking about here is all to do with the importance of being open to understanding how others experience reality.

After spending a great deal of time talking with my new Korean friends, we took a trip to the DMZ line. A year earlier I had travelled to South Korea and there I had got the history lesson from their point of view. But now, standing in a building on the northern side overlooking the border, I could see the line that divided North and South. I could see the North and South Korean soldiers on either side, just as I had from the other side a year before. I remember thinking to myself how similar they looked, dressed in military attire, representing their country. At that moment I realised I was wrong in my assumptions about all I knew of Korea and its history. How wrong? I'm not entirely sure. But I know there's another way of thinking about it.

There's always more than one side to the story. Often, there are many. And this is absolutely critical to understand. The people I met in Korea were brought up and educated to believe certain ideas. I was brought up and educated to believe certain other ideas. I might want to believe I'm right and they might want to believe they're right. In some democratic societies we can debate these ideas, which is wonderful. Yet, at the same time, that doesn't mean we're going to convince other people to believe what we believe.

Richard Dawkins wrote his book *The God Delusion* as an attack on religion. Christians in the United States dismiss such a perspective by stating the inability of science to disprove the existence of God. All faiths have managed to survive despite religious competition and an increasing shift towards atheism around the world. Why? Because we don't rely on truth to justify our beliefs: we make things true to justify them. That's how we do it. I have atheist friends, Christian friends, Muslim friends, Buddhist friends, agnostic friends, Jewish friends, Hindu friends. I never lose an argument about belief with any of them, for one fundamental reason: I never have one.

Beliefs either serve us or harm us. And when they harm me, I will challenge them. When they harm my clients, I will challenge them. But by looking at the world through this filter I am able to see things differently. What you are reading in this book is going to provoke you, challenge you and get you to think. But the most important message we hope will get through is the idea that you are not at the mercy of your beliefs. By believing in more, things can become more wonderful. For example, in North Korea, Cho Hee and Hy were a delight to be around and I connected with them strongly. Together with our driver, Jin, I saw three lovely, genuine people who had wonderful personalities and a really positive view of the world.

The truth is that we all live in a dictatorship when we allow our own beliefs to dictate what we can and cannot do. To truly liberate ourselves we must learn to challenge and question our own philosophy and attitude so that we are in a position from which we can see things differently. How we decide to run our brain can be seen as the government of our mind. Just like governments in the world, we can run our mental economy into the ground and end up, as Richard Bandler would say, with an impoverished model of the world.

As Richard and I sat at the kitchen table in the west of Ireland, I'd been listening to him discuss the early ideas around some of the various parts of the NLP model and I got a really clear insight from what he'd been saying. The real genius in what they accomplished in the very early days was the ability to avoid buying into the assumptions that everyone else seemed to buy into. Instead of allowing themselves to follow traditional and conventional theories, they challenged the very presuppositions of the way change happened. Instead of seeing Gestalt therapy, family therapy or hypnotherapy as having all the answers, they were interested in what was actually being done. As Richard had said, "You don't have to take the beliefs to learn the skills."

But along with those skills came new beliefs. Richard's beliefs in what he could do enabled him to accomplish so many things. His belief in the capacity of human beings for change helped

The Insider's Guide to the Brain

him to get incredible results with people. Often, NLP is described as an attitude, because of the very beliefs that guide it. This paradox is illustrated in the idea that "the map is not the territory". What NLP addresses is the fact that the way we think about something is either useful or not useful, rather than true or false. This differentiation enables us to avoid the trap of trying to be right. This is a trap that we can all too easily fall into.

As I made my way home to the east coast after spending a couple of days with Richard, I saw a sign for a town that read *Straight ahead, 10 miles*. I drove straight ahead for about five miles and came to another sign for the same town that read *Straight ahead, 12 miles*. I laughed in recognition that, in my beautiful country of Ireland, things are rarely as they seem.

I began to listen to the recordings of my conversations with Richard as I drove home. It was exciting. I had begun a fresh new journey and it was more exciting than ever!

Being a white person in North Korea, I was expecting a lot of people to be unwelcome. The second last day I was there, I met an old lady with a beautiful little girl who was her Granddaughter. Instead of looking at me suspiciously and avoiding eye contact, the old lady smiled and the little girl reached up for a hug.

5. RANDOM RAMBLINGS: YOU'RE ABSOLUTELY RIGHT

"YOU'RE RIGHT." When you hear someone say that, it feels good, doesn't it? Being right feels good. Being wrong feels bad. When we get something right, our brain releases feel-good chemicals. Here's the thing: the need to be right can actually make us stupider. By rushing to conclusions, we often miss important bits of information that can help us make more intelligent decisions. Furthermore, when we try and influence others perhaps one of the worst things we can do is to make them feel wrong. It's a really big mistake. So, understanding how to handle these two issues is absolutely critical.

There was a fascinating study conducted by the psychologist Ming Hsu and his team into what happens in the brain when we experience ambiguity or uncertainty. What they found was that the feeling of ambiguity increased activity in the amygdala, the part of the brain responsible for regulating emotions and that factors in when we're preparing ourselves to respond to threats.

The amygdala processes the input received by the brain from the environment in order to evaluate whether or not it's a threat. In the same study Hsu found that the presence of ambiguity also reduced the amount of activity in another part of the brain, the ventral striatum, which is responsible for how we feel when we get rewarded for something. So, uncertainty actually causes us to feel threatened and prevents us from feeling good in many contexts. As David DiSalvo, author of the book *What Makes Your Brain Happy and Why You Should Do the Opposite*, puts it: the brain craves certainty.

The implications for this are easy to see. We strive to be "right" so that we can feel certain and can feel good. You can see this when you're talking to someone who has just successfully predicted their own downfall. Often, as they describe the "I told you I was going to lose" story, they seem to do it with a wry smile accompanying their story. Indeed, it seems that they derive some pleasure from their own pain . . . simply because they were right about it.

This explains, from a neurological point of view, the existence of the "confirmation bias" in psychology. This suggests that if you believe something, you will tend to look for evidence that confirms your theory and tend to dismiss evidence that contradicts it.

A phenomenon in psychology known as "cognitive dissonance" is connected with this. When a person feels conflicted because of a discrepancy between their beliefs and behaviours, they often feel a sense of dissonance and seek to resolve this by changing their beliefs or behaviours.

When it comes to communicating with other people it's essential to be aware of how you can avoid making them "wrong", or at least to take into consideration the negative feeling of them feeling wrong. Of course, there's also how they might feel about being wrong in front of others, which is an extra negative feeling. But the primary negative feeling to watch out for is the one they will have if they find themselves to be wrong.

The language models used in NLP serve to challenge beliefs in such a way that it's the person themselves who uncovers their beliefs. At the same time, you help them build a more useful and resourceful belief that serves to empower them and gives them a replacement sense of certainty. So while they examine their beliefs and discover what isn't a reliable or valid belief, you're opening up their options and giving them the opportunity to believe something else.

Often when people try and influence others they put forward an argument about why the other person is wrong. These arguments usually fall flat, no matter how well articulated they are. The reason is that people will defend even the most irrational beliefs in an effort not to be wrong. So, do your best to help people to feel right and just adjust their belief so it fits a more useful way of thinking.

What we also need to remember is how this theory is relevant to ourselves. One of the things that can continue to limit you is a lack of tolerance towards uncertainty or ambiguity. The key is to become okay with being wrong, so that you can be free to change and adjust based on what the most useful thing to do is. If you allow yourself the room to change your beliefs, your mind is open to a limitless world of possibility.

So, how do you do this? It's actually simpler than you think. It does require practice, but it's only a one-step process. Here's what you do: accept a belief that says you'll sometimes be wrong and then if you're ever wrong you can feel good about the fact that you proved yourself correct.

Believe it or not, this simple cognitive trick has worked wonders for me. Accepting that you're going to be sometimes right and sometimes wrong means that when you're wrong you can remind yourself that you were right about being wrong. Therefore, your brain can still feel good. Also, you can understand that being wrong doesn't necessarily mean that you're under threat. If you plan more strategically you can find that being wrong often actually makes you safer, as it teaches you what you most need to know, which will protect you in future situations. Focusing on the usefulness of making mistakes and being wrong helps you think differently about being right. This way, you can feel right more of the time.

SECTION 2: BRAINS, LANGUAGE AND COMPUTERS

Dublin, Sunday, 24 May 2009

ON A MONDAY EVENING IN MAY 2009, Richard came to Dublin to give a talk. It was really exciting for us to have him back in Ireland. Dublin was where I first saw Richard, in the mid-1990s. His speech back then was the turning point for me and it convinced me of what I wanted to do with my life.

Richard had returned a few times since then. I remember the highlight being when he came over in June 2003 and did a very special seminar, at which Brian Colbert and myself shared the stage with him, entitled "30 Years of NLP: A Guide to Being Happy". Having the experience of training jointly with Richard had been a dream come true.

Now, six years later, I had written a book with him, we had become close friends and he continued to be a fantastic guide and mentor to me. Richard was introduced on stage by myself and Brian. He proceeded to entrance the audience with his fascinating stories and wonderful insights.

The afternoon before, just after he arrived in Dublin, I got a chance to sit down with him in his hotel and discuss more of his memories of the earliest days in NLP. When I arrived I was already excited to see Richard again. It had been months and though I had been listening to the answers he'd given so far, there were many questions still on my mind. I wanted to know more about the discovery of other parts of his life's work. I was interested in understanding the backdrop to Design Human Engineering® and Neuro-Hypnotic Repatterning™, two of his creations. I was curious about how he managed to utilise the background models and skills in such a way that they could help people with specific problems and about how some of the NLP techniques evolved. Most of all, I wanted to explore with Richard what the discovery of NLP meant from a neurological standpoint and what we could do differently as a result.

As I sat down in the lobby, I looked around me at the people meeting in the hotel. I smiled in appreciation of all the brains that communicated with other brains – the billions of neurons that were at work in the very act of communication, the incredible work that goes on between our ears every day. Every single day . . . Then I stopped and realised I was being an ultra-nerd!

6. INNOVATIONS OF THE MIND

SINCE THE CREATION OF NLP we know so much more about neurology, linguistics and computer programming. The computers we have now can do incredible things. We have a more informed understanding of how people use language. The insight we have into how our brains work is far more than it was four years ago, never mind forty years ago.

As the field has developed I have seen two things. I have encountered many books and courses simply repeating the same ideas that were taught back in the 1970s. But I have also seen people like Richard innovate and update the skills of NLP continuously into faster and better ways of doing things. I wanted to hear more from him about the field and, in particular, about what he recommends people should do in order to make sure they're getting the best kind of training in the field.

Richard soon arrived at the hotel and we sat across from each other. After a quick catch-up I placed my iPhone down on the table and started started to record our conversation.

> OF: What are the things to keep in mind when starting to learn NLP? You know, it's one thing to go to somebody like yourself, or someone you've trained and begin to learn NLP, but there are a million different versions of NLP out there – well, what they call NLP, anyway! – with people making complicated models, with this rubbish and that rubbish. So, for somebody who's reading an NLP book for the first time and thinking, I want to do a course, what are the things they should keep in mind when beginning their journey into NLP?
>
> RB: Well, I, of course, have a very strong opinion, because I made up the term! And I made up the term to describe the sets of activities that I was engaging in, which are supposed to do the following things: number 1, they should be simple; and number 2, they should work. So if you're going to learn NLP from somebody, it should fulfil these two criteria.
>
> Your teacher should be able to show you that. He or she should be able to take somebody out of the audience in the first hour and enable that person to change profoundly. Now, if they can't do that, they can't teach you what they don't know.
>
> Now, if they draw infinitely complex things on their charts and tell you terribly circuitous things and tell you that you have to be ultra-smart in order to learn this, be wary! Guess what: I'm not ultra-smart! I'm ultra-practical. When I teach I demonstrate everything that I teach and I show you that it can be done. In fact, I'll show you things you'll never be able to figure out how I'm doing – not because they're hard, but because they're too easy. And the real answers are always those that are blatantly obvious.
>
> Moshé Feldenkrais, who was an amazing physicist that did bodywork, named his book *The Elusive Obvious*. I always loved the title, because once

you know how it works it all seems so simple. Everything in science, music, art – everything I've ever done – when you find out how it works you go, "Wow, that's so simple!"

And when people try to make things unnecessarily complex to impress and intimidate you, using esoteric terminology and equations, that's not what math is for. Math is designed to simplify things, not to mystify things, not to obfuscate. My work is about demystifying things, making knowledge and techniques accessible to all. My book *The Secrets of Being Happy* is a good example of that. It's designed so that anybody can pick it up and fix themselves! And that's what I want. I want simple tools.

It'd be one thing if I was old and dead, but I'm still around and so are most of my best students and we're all members of the same organisation. Now, there are people who have left along the way because they didn't like what I was doing. They thought it wasn't the real stuff, that what I was doing thirty years ago was the real stuff. But what I used to do thirty years ago was just way too hard and complicated. What we're doing now is easier, faster and better.

Because it's a new field it should have a rapid development in the beginning. And everything that we do should be more effective and efficient than what we did ten years ago. If people are still doing what I did thirty years ago, how are they going to get you into the future if they can't go there themselves?

I had seen videos of Richard spanning over thirty years. He was updating the field and he was updating himself. What he was talking about now resonated strongly with me. Somewhere along the way the NLP and coaching industries got lost inside their own frameworks. They kept to the same kind of patterns and techniques but simply made them more complicated and used more challenging vocabulary. To me, this wasn't change.

On the other hand, the true innovations I have witnessed didn't require extra-big words. There was no requirement for additional vocabulary, just a different application of the same skills.

Design Human Engineering®
Design Human Engineering® (DHE) is one of the most creative technologies I have ever come across. One of the ways I think about it is that it allows you to take the best experiences and use them in your imagination.

I remember being on a morning trek in Tikal, the ancient Mayan ruins in the north of Guatemala, lying in the heart of the jungle. It was about six in the morning and we had just reached a high part of the land. I heard very strange and incredibly loud sounds. They sounded like they were coming from a dinosaur. (Seriously, I was convinced that a T-Rex was about to emerge from the forest and I'd be forced to save everyone!) I tried desperately to remember tactics from one of the *Jurassic Park* movies, but, alas, it was to no avail. I'd have to face this monster alone.

Actually, it turned out that the noises I heard were made by howler monkeys – good name for them. They were so loud and the sound was so powerful that I was glad I didn't have to save the day.

The fact that the sound of the monkeys had left such an impression on me made me realise just how many sounds and visions there are in the world that we fail to really use to induce states and feelings. When I visited India for the first time, for example, I found all my senses being overloaded with powerful new sights, sounds, sensations, tastes and smells. Travelling so much made me aware of just how many different kinds of environment there are in the world. The problem is that our own internal environment – our mind – isn't as rich as the external one.

For the most part, we spend our time reflecting on the same worthless images of bad things that have happened in the past or that we anticipate happening in the future. We talk to ourselves in an annoying and irritating voice so that we can criticise ourselves more easily. We spend a lot of time in a mental environment that just isn't good for us. But, by using the richness of the world outside, we can help ensure that our internal world is richer and full of wonderfully good feelings.

DHE is about being creative and coming up with new images and sounds in our head that allow us to feel better and do better. In NLP, if your negative inner voice is telling you that you're ugly, you might try and change this so that it no longer does so. In DHE you replace it with the sexiest voice you can imagine (whatever you find sexy!), saying to yourself, God, you're soooo hot! Mmmmnnn, you're so gorgeous. Seeeexxxyyyy! Now, when you learn to talk to yourself like this, in this tone of voice, it radically changes your state.

The possibilities with DHE are exciting. Not only can you change how you're thinking but you can also generate new kinds of feelings with which you're able to create new chemical cocktails of positive emotions in your mind. I wanted to know more from Richard about how he came up with the idea.

> OF: Could you talk to us about your memories of the origination of Design Human Engineering®?
>
> RB: Well, that's really kind of an odd thing. DHE was something I calculated mathematically. It was the opposite to NLP in many ways. I had elicited zillions of strategies. I got strategies from architects, artists, musicians . . . Everybody I ever met who had any skill, I'd find out how they motivated themselves, what strategy they used to learn things, what strategy they used to present them, what strategies they learnt to decide which one to do – all kinds of detail like that. And at a certain point in time I remember thinking to myself, most of these suck!
>
> A lot of these people motivated themselves with pain and unpleasantness. Even when you got through – and we did streamlining strategies where we tried to cut out the stuff that was just extraneous and make it more efficient – we were able to make strategies better than they were. They were missing the part that I would like, which is that they were enjoyable.
>
> I'd worked for an interior decorator when I was in college, just part time. I would paint some rooms and would do this and that. I remember him talking to this woman, because there was this room with white walls and white carpet and I remember walking in there going, you know, "how bland is this?" And he would start to say:
>
> "We're going to put this there and throw some pillows here" and I remember her going, "well, my husband doesn't like a lot of frivolous stuff." And the interior decorator looked at me and says to her:
>
> "Ma'am, if you can't make this room fun to come in, nobody's ever going to go in here. He'd come in here and sit by himself in some functional chair, but you know you have to tell him that a room doesn't just have to be a room:

it should be fun." And, to me, when you go inside your head it should be the same thing.

When I created Design Human Engineering® I went back and looked at all the piles of equations that I had – and I had books and books of strategies and stuff – and started to ask myself the question, what would be the opposite of this? So instead of using categories like "elegance" (the minimum number of steps to get the maximum results), I started going, what would be the maximum number of steps you could take to get an even better result and have a lot more fun? I set up a whole new set of criteria and literally started designing strategies.

Whereas NLP was sequential elicitation of a strategy and simultaneous installation, DHE was simultaneous elicitation and sequential installation. The force of consciousness allows us to create intelligent designs for what we want inside our head.

Design Human Engineering® went like this: in your imagination, instead of having one voice that told you to do something, imagine a whole backing choir of three hundred people singing, like you would in a Gospel church. I literally went through a phase of going out with my holophonic mics and discovering stuff like that and putting it all in a big sampler – which now would be a small sampler, but in those days was literally something the size of a desk and that was only a gigabyte of memory!

I remember getting that first GB disc and it was about three feet across and I'm thinking, wow, this is really small. And then designing strategies so that when people think inside their heads they had the sound of lions roaring with strength and gospel choirs telling them to get up and go do it. And it was fun to do that. And my clients liked it better. The great thing about Design Human Engineering® is that you can use this wonderful installation where every sound that exists on the planet becomes a tool. I went with Denver Clay and I recorded absolutely every sound. We went everywhere and everything went to use for something.

Why should you just memorise McDonald's commercials? We have this wonderful tape recorder in our head and if you start putting trumpets in the right place you become uplifted. The funny thing I do in seminars – of playing fanfare trumpets like the king is coming in and getting guys to do that in their mind when they unzip their pants – changes your attitude.

Having great music, great sounds and big, beautiful pictures where you need them propels you. Just the fact that a picture is moving forward in your head makes you feel like you're moving already. Static images don't produce movement in your body. It's not just that you have a big screen: if you can make it a three-dimensional screen, 360 degrees and 40 feet high and all these wonderful things we started doing, then you can impact how someone feels more.

NLP was all about pulling these strategies out of one person and sticking them in another. DHE, on the other hand, became something where you became much more of an artist. You looked at what was there and went, "It's not enough" and built something dramatic and wonderful and exciting that was good enough.

In many ways this is also why I was no longer interested in well-formed outcomes but instead my focus was on well-formed directions. It's not about just doing something better but having a whole new improvement in your quality of life.

Since I first learnt to use DHE I have made the inside of my mind a wonderful place to live. When I need motivation, an orchestra and choir play in my mind and propel me towards doing what I need to do. When I want to feel cool and relaxed, I hear rap music in my mind and I walk with a stride. When I want to feel confident, I imagine an audience smiling at me, cheering and clapping for me and whispering audibly to each other, "He's so amazing. He's so good." They help me to feel incredible when I most need to.

Neuro-Hypnotic Repatterning™
Another of Richard's technologies is known as Neuro-Hypnotic Repatterning™ (NHR). This is one of the most important developments in how he helps people to make changes in the way they feel and what they do. NHR describes a process whereby you use hypnosis to alter the neurological pattern of various problems and change the chemistry of your mind.

Every negative state carries with it a particular strategy that was used to create that state. For example, if a person feels depressed it's because they're making images and talking to themselves in ways that create a negative feeling of depression. Once you're aware of this strategy for becoming and remaining depressed, you can change it.

NHR enables you not only to work on the strategy but also to examine the structure of the actual feeling itself. It examines how the subjective experience of the feeling works. Whenever a person feels a particular feeling, it begins somewhere in their body and then moves somewhere else and it usually goes in a particular direction. When you can help that person to re-access that feeling, to notice its direction so that you can get them to reverse the direction it goes in or spins in, they will find themselves feeling completely different.

You see, what happens is this: by getting the person who has been feeling bad to change the way they experience the actual sensations, you can make them change the feeling. When you change the feeling, you can't feel it in the same way, because you have connected it chemically with another experience. So, neurologically, whenever you run the feeling backwards the chemical structure of the feeling will alter.

If your brain chemistry is working in a particular way and you use your mind to change it, it will work differently. You have the ability inside your head to release good chemicals. It simply requires you to think in new ways. When you do so, you will be able to release the chemicals that make you feel good and that have a good impact on your brain.

At the same time, NHR enables you to experience really good feelings even more strongly by spinning them or moving them in the same direction as before. You can take good feelings you have had, focus on how they manifested themselves in your body and have them move through the same sequences as before.

This is true even with drug states you've experienced. If you've ever experienced a drug sensation – legal or illegal – your body is what generated the good feeling. Your body knows how. The good feeling you get isn't from the drug itself but from your body's response to it. Your ability to generate feelings is largely untapped. NHR looked at the fact that when you experience a drug, the feeling and sensation starts somewhere and then moves in a particular direction in your body. So if you imagine the same sensations vividly, you can create the same kinds of feelings.

Brains, Language and Computers

I asked Richard about the discovery of NHR.

RB: Well, that's kind of a funny thing, Neuro-Hypnotic Repatterning™. I've always gone through phases where I do a whole lot of hypnosis and then I've got to go off and do other things and then I'll come back to it again and again. I had an opera singer years and years and years ago who hired me because he was having some sort of nasal problem. His nose ran all the time and the doctors started telling him it was some kind of mental thing. I don't know what it was. But when I saw the guy, I had done something with somebody where I had hypnotised them and had them walking through the desert for two weeks. It was only, like, thirty minutes – time distortion, all that. When they came out, their sinuses were dry and their lips were dry. I was going to do something like that with this guy.

I came to meet him and said, "Tell me what you want me to do exactly" and the guy started. He used the intonation that you hear when someone says, "Got your nose, little Johnny" and he said, "Well, something's wrong with my nose." And I heard that melody and I literally reached over and went, "Here's your nose back" and just touched him on the nose. He jerked his head back and when he started talking he had no stuffed up nose at all. I'd been there three minutes.

I literally said to him, "What can you do to make your nose run?" and he said, "Well, if I start practising this aria it will start running immediately." And he went in the other room for fifteen minutes and he came out and goes, "It's not running!" I think somebody just did this hypnotic thing when he was a little kid and forgot to give him his nose back and his unconscious did something goofy with it. I don't know. That's my guess, but I could be wrong.

Anyway, his nose worked fine and he paid me an enormous amount of money. I mean, just an *enormous* amount of money. I said, "Is there anything else I can do for you?" and he goes, "Well, I have trouble motivating myself to practise." And I said, "All the time?" And he said, "Well, sometimes." And I said, "What's the difference? When you feel motivation, where does it start?" And he points to his stomach. I said, "The times you actually get up, where does it go?" He says, "Well, being an opera singer, it goes up to my throat" and he made a gesture where his hands came out and started cycling forward. I said, "Cool. And?" "Well, sometimes I can't do that." And as soon as he said that, he rotated his hands in the opposite direction. And I remember thinking, this is going to be easy.

So I put him in a trance and had him get up and say whatever he said that made it hard. But I had him literally move his hands and spin the feelings in the same old direction. When I brought him out of trance he only had to make this hand gesture and suddenly he felt motivated.

We'd had people go into trance and you could put them in hypnosis and get them drunk and when we did elicitation with them you could induce drug states in people. I remember Ed Reese did it with somebody for Demerol® – a seventy-year-old lady who had never taken any drugs since she'd been in the hospital. He had her go through and remember where she first felt Demerol®

and literally induced drug states again by going through four or five locations on the body where she felt the effects of the narcotic.

I remember taking some guy that used to smoke pot and I said, "Where's the first place you feel it?" and then the second place and the third place and have him go back until he could remember a sequence of five or six things. And the guy got so high, because the only time your consciousness is moved in that particular order is when you took the drug. So when you go and focus on those locations in that sequence, back to the beginning and keep doing it over and over again, it's not the drug that gets you high, it's your body's response to it.

The only time the body has previously run through that sequence is in that altered state, so as they run through that sequence a lot of people re-experience whatever the effect of the narcotic or the drug was. Somewhere in my mind I started putting those two things together. Even in *The Structure of Magic*, I said I was going to do three things. In that book I literally stated in the beginning that I was going to look at change in terms of the individual, how personal history affects us; number 2, the social aspects, like language; and number 3, the neurological things.

The more we learnt about neurology, the more I read about neurology; I realised that a big part of the change has to do with how you go into an altered state. It changes your body chemistry and therefore affects your neurology. So I got the idea: what if we were to bathe people in certain chemical states? Instead of bathing you in a narcotic, we could bathe you in serotonin. And if we could recapitulate that, now, having done lots of research where I looked at people's states of consciousness – in brainwave machines and mind mirrors and EEG machines and things – I knew what brainwave patterns looked like.

In order to alter your state you have to change your body chemistry. If we could induce the right state of consciousness and get people to bathe themselves in that neurology, then we could make powerful changes.

It turns out it works extremely well. In the classes I do in Neuro-Hypnotic repatterning™ we spend a lot of time teaching people to go into very deep states and from those deep states how to bathe themselves in just the right neuro-chemistry. This is not just about pain control or something like that: it's another side of the same coin.

You can change your conscious mind a lot, but you can also change more of your state. All of the hollow and solid organs in the body and the intestines have between them neuro-connections called the enteric nervous system. There's a kind of confusion between whole-body sensations and the enteric nervous system that we call emotional responses. Learning to direct that, much the way the opera singer did – so that you could spin your feelings on purpose in one direction or another, or some combination of those – allows us to bathe ourselves in a certain set of feelings and then think different ideas so that we can re-programme our mind.

DHE and NHR are not complicated methodologies. They are simply innovations based on what has gone before and what has been found to work better now. Their discovery led to a better understanding of what you could do with the brain.

Richard had emphasised the importance of practicality in everything he did. What I always found was that he would be far more likely to demonstrate a skill than to talk about it endlessly. He firmly believed that you learn best by doing and practising. This was evident in the number of techniques that were developed, from the earliest days of NLP. The various individuals who were around in the early days and who learnt from the co-creators were taught to have an attitude that was focused on practically applying the models or skills on people to help them with problems. I wanted to get a better understanding of how some of the techniques in the field came about.

7. SOFTWARE FOR THE MIND: POWERFUL TECHNIQUES FOR LIFE CHANGE

A HAND WENT UP TO VOLUNTEER for the "fast phobia cure". It was at a seminar in England, an NLP teaching practitioner course I was training with my friend and colleague Kate Benson. It is one of the most powerful techniques and was designed to help you change your association of something that terrified you so that you could feel okay about it. The first time I heard of it I thought it was rubbish – until I experienced it myself, that is. I remember, on the second-last day of my first NLP practitioner course, having the phobia cure tested. They brought in snakes and spiders for all those who were afraid of these two creatures, including me. To my surprise, I found myself handling both by the end of the day, feeling relaxed. I found myself experiencing results that changed how I thought about what was possible.

The technique works by guiding a person into using their imagination to see themselves watching themselves experience the phobia while sitting in a cinema auditorium. Then you have them imagine themselves floating out of their body into the projection booth so that they can see themselves sitting in the cinema watching themselves on screen. This makes them feel ultra-safe and secure as the movie runs on. Next, you have them float into the end of the movie, when everything is okay again and you get them to run the movie backwards so that they walk backwards, talk backwards and experience everything backwards. They do this, to the very beginning of the movie, a number of times. Afterwards, when they think about what frightened them, they feel removed from the fear. The feeling just isn't the same and they find themselves feeling significantly better about what used to provoke fear. It's quite a powerful technique.

At the seminar, I signalled to the volunteer, Catherine, to come up on stage for the demonstration and we began. As Catherine sat down on the stage I asked her what she was afraid of.

She replied, "A bridge near where I live. I can't drive across it. I haven't been able to in years."

I said, "Do you need to be able to cross it?"

She replied, "My grandson lives across the other side of it, so I only get to see him when he visits me. But it's just too hard. I know it's silly, logically, but when I even consider approaching it I imagine that, as I'm on it, it begins to collapse into the river below."

Now, if there's one habit I've got into it's that of always trying to work with every problem in a different way. There would be plenty of time to do the fast phobia cure. But first I wanted to explore what she had just said. Most people I meet who have phobias about crossing a bridge worry about two irrational things: falling off the bridge or the bridge collapsing. It occurred to me that this was fairly predictable and not very interesting. But I had an idea. "That seems kind of boring, don't you think?" I replied. She looked at me with a puzzled expression on her face.

"I mean, a bridge collapsing. Boooring! A bit obvious, isn't it? I mean, if you're going to scare yourself you may as well do it properly. Be a bit creative."

Her bewilderment slowly gave way to a half smile.

I continued, "Here's what I want you to do: close your eyes for a second."

She did so and prepared to visualise.

"Now, I want you to imagine that you're approaching the bridge and as you start to cross it, it begins to shake and slowly starts to collapse. But this time, as it does so, an alien comes down from the planet Zygor, gets into the passenger seat beside you and stabs you in the right eye with a compass. So, as your car falls into the river, the inside of the car fills up with the blood cascading from your eyeball. Before you even hit the water, you drown in your own blood."

As she imagined this ridiculously crazy scenario she couldn't help but laugh at how mad it was. I'm pretty sure she was even more convinced of my apparent weirdness. But here's the best part: when I asked her to think about crossing the bridge from then on, all she could do was laugh. From that moment, every time she imagined crossing the bridge, she saw the alien, the compass and the silly scenario. And because it was so over the top, the feeling of fear dissipated.

The brain tends to remember what stands out the most, what is strangest. This is known in psychology as the "salience effect". By having Catherine imagine the experience in a radically new and far more action-packed way, I was able to make the new memory stand out even more effectively. The key was to replace the old movie with a new imaginary scenario that was ridiculous enough to make her feel differently.

Whenever I work with clients I'm always focused on helping them change the way they feel, not only about whatever they feel bad about, or frightened of, but also about the fact that they feel bad or frightened. I believe most people's worst problem isn't the problem itself: it's the problem that they have with the problem.

The key is to repattern in their mind how they feel about the experience so that it no longer carries the same feeling when they think about it. My work with Catherine was my own innovation, which was based on a different way of thinking about problems. Whenever I've seen Richard work with a client, he always does what he can to get them to think differently about the problem. From his creativity came a number of really great NLP techniques.

As I will discuss below, with NLP I had learnt to help people change the way they thought about the past by means of "change personal history", to become more motivated through the "Godiva Chocolate pattern" and to overcome compulsions using the "threshold pattern". I was curious about how these techniques came about and wanted to question Richard about his memories of their evolution.

Changing personal history

The first technique I was curious about is known as "change personal history". In it you go inside your mind and recall a negative event you feel bad about. You then access a really good feeling and anchor it. Next, you go back in your mind to before the negative event occurred and you fire off the positive feeling so that you can go through that past negative event with a new, more resourceful feeling. It helps the feeling associated with the memory change so that you think about the past experience differently.

> OF: Some of the work that you've taught me includes how to change the way people think about past events. Where did the idea of change personal history come from?

RB: Well, the idea for this really came from Virginia Satir more than anyone else! I can't take credit for that myself. That was what Virginia did in almost all of her therapy. She had people go back and she would change what happened. Virginia would have them relive old events, but what would change is that people would verbalise the reasons why they did something. Even though they weren't alive any more, she would have other people play their parts. She would set up things that had gone on three generations back so that, if you really knew what people were thinking at the time, it would be different. It affects your feelings kinaesthetically. It alters the generalisations and beliefs you have about it.

So we formalised it. We didn't need thirty people to play all your family members that were dead. We just had you do it inside your head and go back. You had a crappy childhood? Put in something good.

The other person that should get credit for that is Milton Erickson. He age-regressed people. There was a famous case of his where a woman grew up without a mother and she knew nothing about having sex, so she was terrified of having sex! She was an adult woman about to get married or something.

Milton went into her history and he appeared as the February Man or something. He appeared to her periodically in a state and would inform her of all the things she didn't know about sex. So when she woke up she could go back in her history and have this wealth of experience based on what he had told her. So rather than being afraid of the future, she wasn't.

And she's not the only one. They did psychodrama where they got people to replay times from the past and act it out so they could change what happened. Lots of the psychotherapies had something where you went back into the past and relived something differently.

I was just official about it. I said, "Why fool around?" You go into your mind, you go back into your history, you alter the pictures and you feel differently. If that gives you more freedom, then that's fine. I don't really do it much any more; I don't think it's necessary. I'm more interested in the future. I believe the best thing about the past is that it's over. I keep reiterating that.

Those techniques were what we formalised out of psychotherapy; it's what psychotherapy was kind of all about. Once things evolved over the years, all of that stuff became unnecessary, if interesting. If I want to change something horrible from someone's past, I'm interested in changing the way they feel about it. A bad past experience can make you weak, or it can make you stronger. I heard on the news recently that if you live through horrible things, they can only make you stronger. That might be nice, but it's not reality!

Some people go through terrible things and it cripples them for the rest of their life. I can't even imagine the suffering of the people in Austria who were found in 2008 in a basement where a man had imprisoned his daughter for twenty-four years. Here she was sexually assaulted repeatedly by her father and afterwards a number of her children were taken away. Three of her children have done little more than watch television and eat. They've never been out in the sunlight.

They could use a little "change history". But what they really need is new old history so that they can cope with the outside world. Now, given the amount of television they've watched, you could probably have them put some of those memories inside their head and use them so that they knew how to talk to and be around, other people. Instead of living their whole life disassociated you could get them to associate with better memories than the ones they have.

What your personal history does is prepare you for dealing with the future. And the techniques I use now teach people how to deal with the future with more immediacy than is possible by going and lying to yourself about the past.

Before I trained in NLP I had studied hypnotherapy and hypnoanalysis in particular. Part of this approach involved my using hypnosis to help people go into their past and relive traumatic experiences in the hope that, by experiencing them again, they would release these negative feelings. Time and time again I found that simply having them relive the same experiences over and over again never really helped much. It was only when I helped them change how they thought or felt about such experiences that they reported feeling a lot better.

I soon found out that what I had been doing intuitively was a natural part of NLP. Helping a person feel differently about bad memories or traumatic experiences was an area where NLP came in particularly useful and I've found myself using it with thousands of people in therapy since I did my very first NLP practitioner course.

Discussing the change history technique with Richard was particularly fascinating, given the name of this book, as we were actually talking about the idea of changing our memories. The reality, though, is that our memories always distort what really happened. For example, I have seen a number of instances where people have recalled the early days of NLP. Despite there being some overlap, I've heard many different versions of the same event. You have some people who collaborate with their versions, but the truth is that their realities have already been transformed by what actually happened since then.

It's like the book you're reading. To the best of our memories, what we describe about our past experiences is as accurate as possible, but time itself and a bunch of cognitive biases, will no doubt have distorted them. Indeed, if you check Wikipedia for "memory biases" you will find no fewer than fifty-two different ways in which our memories are subject to distortion!

The beauty of distorting or adding to memories on purpose lies in your ability to change the way you think and feel about your past in a way that empowers you. Since you can't be 100 per cent sure about your recollection of events, it's a smart idea to recall events in a way that serves you. Instead of leaving this up to the natural flaws in our recall system, you get to use your imagination to construct things slightly differently and improve how you feel.

Godiva chocolate pattern
Being able to do something about the past was terrifically useful to me. But I was also interested in learning how to do something about the future. One of the most important factors in deciding whether or not someone succeeds in their life is motivation. In my early years of learning NLP I was introduced to a pattern known as the "Godiva Chocolate pattern." Now, at the time I had never tried Godiva chocolate, so it didn't make much sense to me, but the actual technique worked wonders.

Basically, it involves going inside your mind and thinking about something you crave. (The name of the technique came from the fact that many people craved that kind of chocolate!). Once you've done this you then think about something you want to feel motivated to do. Now you have two images: what you crave (e.g. ice-cream) and what you want motivation for (e.g. getting up early).

The technique involves taking the image of getting up early and putting it into the same location, with the same submodalities, as the image of ice-cream, so that you start to feel the same way about getting up early as you do about ice-cream! It helps you feel the same amount of motivation for the thing that you need to feel compelled to do. I asked Richard about this interesting pattern.

> OF: Where did the Godiva chocolate pattern come from?
> RB: That was a re-anchoring technique from years and years ago. The idea came from something I did to a window once. I had a window that looked out onto something horrible, so I put a sticker on it of something nice. So when I was gazing at the window I was really looking at the sticker! I did this inside my head with an image – taking a bad image and distorting it away like that and putting something new on the top and popping it forward. When I did it in my head, I thought, this could really work!
>
> Basically, I would get the person to imagine the thing that they had the greatest fetish for: Godiva chocolates, money, whatever – it didn't matter. I got them to imagine it and feel whatever wonderful feelings they had about it. I took the image of the thing that they really liked and I pushed it way off in the distance and I tied rubber bands to the four corners, stuck the sticker of the thing that they wanted to be motivated to do over the front, then let go of the rubber bands so that it would pop back into place.
>
> The quicker you pop an image in, the more apt it is to stick there. I don't know why that's the case, but it is the case. That's the foundation of all change patterns like this. By doing this with their fetishes they started to feel a craving for the actions that they needed to feel more motivation for.

Compulsion threshold pattern
Since I had just asked Richard about building a compulsion in order to take action, I wanted to find out more about one of the ways in which he helped people to overcome non-useful compulsions.

> OF: How did you first start working with compulsions?
> RB: Well, one of the things psychiatrists disliked was compulsives. The reason is that they called them all night long on the phone and whined. If you asked them who the most difficult patients were, they didn't say losing weight or quitting smoking – they never even said schizophrenics (because the schizophrenics are locked up with no telephone). They all said compulsives, but I don't think that it's the hardest. Psychiatrists didn't understand how lucky you were to have a patient that did everything you said in detail. They just never gave them enough to do. Some of the first compulsives I had had zillions of compulsions and some of them just had one stupid compulsion.
>
> One person's compulsion was actually chocolate. This person would eat chocolate to the point of being jaundiced. She lived in Toronto, where, at times, it was forty-below at night; but if she saw a piece of candy advertised on television she had to go straight out and get it. Or, worse, her husband did!
>
> I remember vividly wondering how much chocolate they could actually take. Are they going to eat chocolate to the point where it's going to kill them? But they have to do it slowly, for if they ate all that chocolate at once there was an element of saturation. They used to take people who smoked and

put them in a room and make them smoke six packs of cigarettes in an hour so that they never, ever wanted one again.

But I think if you start with your mind and change it there, the change in the outside world is pretty easy.

So, anyway, I had the woman think of her favourite chocolate bar. We were sitting there in front of the fireplace and she was beaming from ear to ear as she fantasised over her favourite fix.

I said, "Now, it's just not big enough" and I asked her how far away it was from her. I think she said 4 or 5 feet in front of her. I had her move it back another 4 or 5 feet but make it a hundred times bigger. It was expanding to where it was a candy bar the size of a skyscraper, looming over her. I asked her what she thought of it now.

She said, "It's kind of frightening now."

I said, "Then watch it fall right on you!"

She literally screamed and afterwards when I asked her to think about chocolate, all she saw was a field of brown. I started showing her pictures from magazines and I had chocolate bars in the refrigerator – her favourite kind, actually. When I pulled them out she was very indifferent and said she just didn't care.

I had elicited from people how they had previously given up compulsions and it all had to do with being fed up with it. You know, instead of thinking about their next candy bar, they'd sit there and think about all the candy bars that they had eaten that they shouldn't have: "And I just kept seeing them and seeing them until I said to myself, enough is enough!" And they'd always make a gesture, with their hands fully extended, like they were looking at a picture the size of a wall.

I'd use that knowledge. I would always find out what people would do to get over their problems and I would go back to my clients with this. The biggest mistake psychology made was to look in the wrong place for the answers! They would take a room full of people who are depressed – these are the only people who don't know how to get over depression, so they don't have the answer! If people couldn't tell their fantasies from reality they would take a whole bunch of them and study them! Or they'd study a control group who never had the problem. What they should have done is find somebody who had the problem but got over it and find out what they did! I did that with a hundred phobics. I had to interview a thousand to get a hundred real ones, but the hundred real ones all did roughly the same thing. That's part of where the disassociation notion came from in the first place.

That's what the compulsion blowout was: I found people who had got over compulsions and I found out what they did and then made it even more dramatic and even bigger. That's one of the reasons why it works so effectively. Compulsives and obsessive-compulsives are very much alike in the sense that they're thorough. If you occupy their time as much with getting over their problem as with good stuff, then they start "cheating" and not doing the bad stuff. You get them compulsively doing things to have fun. Then they won't call you on the phone in the middle of the night.

One of my favourite parts of using NLP is the fact that, despite having great techniques such as these, it offers you many different choices about how to work with past negative feelings, motivation and bad habits. Indeed, since the time of NLP's origins, people have been creating new ways to use the basic skills. While some seem obsessed with turning every version of the same technique into a "brand-new technique" that they invented, the reality is that having a bunch of techniques to help people is like having a bunch of chat-up lines. You need to understand how the process works. Having had Richard explain the various processes, I was able to see how NLP actually helped you to programme your brain more effectively.

Most of the problems people seem to have exist either in their past or in their future. If you can help people feel differently about the past it is extremely powerful. For people to be helped with their future they need to be able to accomplish two feats: they need to be able to do more of what works for them and less of what doesn't. Changing habits and overcoming compulsions helps them do less of what holds them back; building motivation helps them do more of what ensures they succeed. So, that's the past and the future looked at. The next question I had concerned the present and our own ability to start getting our brain working in the best possible way.

8. PIMP YOUR BRAIN

WHENEVER I GO TO SEE Richard he always says at least one thing that makes me burst out laughing and say, "Cool!" One such instance was when he introduced the idea of "pimping your own brain" at a seminar in Italy I was attending. Now that I had the chance, I wanted to ask him more about this wonderful concept.

OF: You mentioned before the seminar the importance of being able to "pimp your brain". Could you elaborate on that?

RB: By "pimp your brain" I don't mean whore it out. What I mean is... there is a TV show where they talk about "pimping your ride", where you go in and they take old broken-down cars and they repaint them and put in fancy upholstery and sometimes they put a popcorn machine in the back because the person likes going to the movies – the drive-in movies – where you make your car so it's totally unique to you and ultra-fancy. So instead of it having the same engine that every car like yours has, you supercharge it and you get better gas mileage and more power and special tyres and special suspension.

When I was a teenager we used to take $30–40 cars from the junkyard and by the time we were done with them they'd be the fastest car around, with the fanciest paint job. We'd put big tyres and chrome wheels on them and we'd paint them. And, you know, we did the work ourselves, so it didn't cost a lot of money. Your brain is the most important tool you have to succeed in all aspects of life – in your relationships, in your work, in your hobbies.

Take the myth that spelling is a genetic phenomenon. Spelling isn't genetic: if you have the right strategy in your brain everybody can spell. If you think about things differently you learn different ways of making pictures and making them more vivid or more detailed.

Same goes for motivation. If people try to motivate themselves with little, tiny pictures – rather than big, detailed pictures – it's very difficult. Some people try to motivate themselves with blurry pictures. It just doesn't work. You have to be able to run advertisements in your head to get yourself to do stuff.

It's just after New Year's and I'm really shocked at how people talk about New Year's resolutions.

One of the people on the news said that it was only ten days after New Year's and she'd already broken her New Year's resolutions. So she can make a decision to change her life and it only has a shelf-life of less than two weeks. I mean, that's ludicrous.

You should be able to know how to make decisions that you stick to and what the difference is in your own brain. Everybody's made a decision that they've stuck to. It looks, it feels, it sounds, it smells, it tastes different than the ones you don't stick to. So if you really want to stick to something, you should know where to put it in your brain and how to construct it. That's what NLP is all about.

NLP is about pimping your brain; it's about customising your thought patterns; it's about being the interior designer of your thought processes so that . . . if you need to motivate yourself rather than try to do it with a groggy, defeated voice, you got trumpets and bold voices telling you to get up and exercise *now* so that you do, rather than going, well, maybe not today and you start putting things off.

It's that old adage: procrastinators never wait to procrastinate. So therefore they have something that's immediate and if they used that for other things then they'd just do those things rather than not do the things that they really want to. And there isn't a heavy emphasis put on thinking in our school systems, or psychology. People think all of these things are inherited rather than being like muscles: you exercise them, you get stronger.

The more ways you learn to use your brain, the more states of consciousness you learn to go in. And let's face it: we just don't have twenty years to sit around Tibet and learn to be relaxed. So we need the tools. This is why I've developed things like the mind spa and the new brain-fit machines, so people can alter their state.

Most of the technology I've developed has come from travelling around the world, where I've seen all these shamans who have procedures that work, if you have enough time. But they're adapted to where they are. They have a week to do a ritual in the Amazon to solve a problem. We don't. We need faster tools that adapt to the way we live in this world. And that's what most of the procedures I've developed are. They're things that work and work right away.

I made a mental note to ask Richard more about altered states and his shamanic experiences at a later date. For now, though, I wanted to continue hearing from him about how to generate the very best states, especially considering the challenges that we face at the present time.

Making your brain a wonderful place to live in is so important because it's your brain or nervous system that interprets whatever happens in the world. Your mind dictates how you experience your reality. So, in many ways, it's your home. The mental environment you create is also largely decided by you. Whereas in the outside world you can grow up in poverty or luxury, in the inner world you can choose where you want to live.

Richard's point was that being motivated, being relaxed, being able to make good decisions, being able to spell – pretty much anything we want to get better at – is down to how we operate our brain. Pimping our brains is such a cool concept because it gives us a vivid sense of how we need to think about our mind.

You see, if you're thinking about "being positive", it can sometimes seem pretty boring. I mean, "think positive, be happy" is so overdone at the moment that there isn't such a positive ring to it. Indeed, the plethora of coaches out there is actually depressing, because there is so little substance in their proclamations.

On the other hand, getting to pimp your brain creates such enticing imagery that it's something far more desirable. It promises that you can make your brain work a lot better than it does. Part of what does this is learning to build the right kind of feelings in your mind. Richard continued by talking about one such feeling: cheerfulness.

RB: People ask me all the time, "How do you become more cheerful?" It's quite simple: you banish bad thoughts and you amplify good thoughts. If you have a voice inside your head that you're enjoying, you make it louder; if you have a voice that's making you feel bad, you shut the fuck up! If you have a feeling in your body that's making you tense, you reverse it and spin it the other way and relax.

Look at your decisions so that your decisions don't start and stop, stop and start – "Well, I want to eat this, but I shouldn't (yadda, yadda. . .)" – make a decision and stick to it! "I'm going to eat one piece of pizza and stop." And then you eat it and you stop and you feel really good about stopping and you make the feeling really powerful so you have something to be happy about.

If you decide to clean a cupboard, you start cleaning it and you feel better and better until it's done and then you feel great. Then you move on to the next thing. Most people say, "If I did this, then I'd be happy." And even if they did it they still wouldn't be happy, because they don't realise that the closer you get to your goals, the better it should feel. And then you can turn and make a new goal and keep building it up.

As I listened to Richard, I found myself sharing his view that proper change resides in taking charge of how you think inside your head. By going in and adjusting how you speak to yourself and by changing the images, you can change the feelings. Really simple NLP. But it works. And it works because it's really powerful.

The following day Richard delivered his talk in front of hundreds of people in the heart of Dublin. He entertained them with the beginnings of NLP and some of the basic skills that made the biggest difference to people. He discussed his different approaches to problems and gave examples of some of the work that influenced him greatly.

He talked about some of his work with schizophrenics and reminisced about the time he worked with a schizophrenic who believed he was Jesus Christ. On hearing this, Richard went into the man's room with two big beams of wood, long nails and a measuring tape and started measuring him for the cross. After a few minutes of Richard building the cross, the man started telling him he wasn't really Jesus but only pretending to be. It was an effective way of getting through to the patient. Stories like these that Richard told of the early days were my favourite.

The day before, as we finished up our conversation, I asked him one more question about what inspired him to work in a different kind of way.

OF: Richard, one of the things that most impacts people when they meet you is your ability to think differently about a person's problem. For example, all the work you've done in helping people who suffer from schizophrenia. What gave you the idea to do something different from what everyone else was doing?

RB: I didn't know any better. As far as I could tell from viewing the field of psychology, they didn't have an approach to treatment, period, other than letting people just talk and sometimes a little bit of using reward and punishment to reinforce behaviours. There was no systematic idea except for John Rosen. Rosen actually had a higher success rate. He was the one that moved them into the house with him and tortured them about their form of schizophrenia. He was very Freudian in his approach but not very Freudian in his actions. He accused the patients of having transference and depended that they take their clothes off and have sex with him right on the spot, especially if they were prudish and wouldn't do it and then he'd chase them around the house – to get them out of that psychiatric mode.

The amazing thing to me when I first went into mental hospitals was the lingo that the psychiatrists and patients shared and the fact that the patients were more adept at it than the psychiatrists. I mean, patients would talk all this psychiatric jargon to me. It really all appeared to me the way [Gregory] Bateson had described it to me.

He said that when you go into mental hospitals the only thing the psychiatrists are in charge of is whether people could get out of them or not. For the rest of it the patients are running the system from the nurses. And as much as some of the patients are persecuted by it, they play into the system and they even comment on it while they're doing it. I mean literally. There was a patient named Brenda and Brenda looks at me one day and says, "Do you want to see me scare him?" and points to the psychiatrist sitting right next to us. She could have reached out and touched either one of us. And she talked about him as if he wasn't even there and then says to him, "The entities were talking about you last night" and the shrink turns around and said, "There are no entities." And she goes, "They said you were going to say that" and started hammering him like that until he started talking about getting her narcotics.

Since she was locked in a padded cell, her only escape was narcotics and she knew how to get to the psychiatrist. And she had gotten herself stuck in there. She even told me how she had got there. She had said that she had lied and that she was drinking her own piss so the nurse would pull her out of a ward where she was being beaten up by the other girls that were in there. It was the only escape hatch she could have. She knew the system so well that she knew what to tell the nurse to get locked in a private room.

Once she was in there, though, she couldn't get out and she was down to two cigarettes a day. She would light them and they watched her and gave her a match so she wouldn't burn herself. She had some scars on her from being in a fire sometime and she had told the shrinks that it was self-inflicted and I asked her, "Was it?" and she said, "No, I don't think so. It was an accident. But that's what they want to hear." And they believed that if they said stuff like that, somehow or other this was going to get them out of it, but actually it was building a deeper hole. When I listened to this kind of stuff going on – and some of them were really out of the zone – I couldn't tell if they were crazy. So was the hospital making them crazy? I had no way to tell. So part of the things I did was to drive them into sanity.

That was Rosen's theory. He wanted to drive schizophrenics sane. He figured, as Virginia did, that the way in which they interact in the family system can actually significantly affect their psychological well-being. Her approach was a system. So when I went there I wasn't even a therapist, so I couldn't do that sort of thing. But when I got families to give me authorisation – especially in private hospitals, where I could pretty much do anything I wanted as long as I had lawyers and the family behind me – I could drive people into states of sanity by making their craziness something they were terrified of.

Brains, Language and Computers

Once again, the innovations of the mind came from not accepting the understood "truths" about psychology and "psychological illnesses". The very beliefs that people had about problems served to limit their ability to get over them. Whether it was in working with schizophrenics by entering their reality and changing it, or in working with people who had bad habits or fears or who lacked motivation, Richard was focused on helping people change how they thought by changing what they experienced inside their mind. It was simple yet profound.

I was interested in how Richard thought about the need to apply such ideas in the modern world, considering how many challenges seemed to rear their ugly heads in the last couple of years. But that would have to wait. We finished up and I met Richard the following evening before his speech and listened to even more memories of what had been made possible through the magic of a unique brain.

The wink ... with an Irish cap!

9. RANDOM RAMBLINGS: SNAKES AND MISTAKES

ONCE IN A WHILE THE MISTAKES you make can come back and bite you! A few years ago I was called on the phone by an English television production company and asked whether I was interested in working with them on a programme about phobias. I said, "Sure" and flew over to London to record the pilot.

We had arranged for me to work with a woman called Maggie who had a phobia about snakes. For the process, I suggested that they get a snake from the pet shop that we could use as a test for the client. When I arrived I was confronted with two challenges.

Firstly, the client I was to work with, who worked for the production company, was terrified of snakes – a really intense, "flaming" phobia. Even worse, she really didn't want to overcome the phobia and was just going through the motions as a big favour to the production team.

The second challenge was that the snake didn't come with a handler. Normally, when snakes are rented out for reasons such as these a snake-handler is provided, but since the production team didn't inform the shop's owner about why they wanted a snake, he just assumed that there was no need. So, we had a snake in a box. I had to be the handler.

The plan was to have Maggie come into the room and to have me holding the snake so that we could get some "before" footage. Then we'd put the snake away and I'd work with her, before bringing it back at the end. It was perfect. Except I had no idea how to hold a snake. I mean, I'd held a snake once before with a snake-handler beside me telling me what to do, but I didn't really listen to what he was saying. It didn't occur to me that I'd ever have to remember his advice. I wasn't thinking, oh, yeah, in case a snake comes into the training-room next week, I should know what to do!

Anyway, I picked up the snake with both hands and it curled around and around, obviously uncomfortable. It was like holding a baby that really didn't want to be there. The lights were on, the camera was rolling and Maggie entered the room. I looked up and smiled as she froze at the door, staring on in terror. I tried to calm her nerves by introducing the snake. "Hi there, this is Daisy the Snake. She's a feisty one." Naming the snake usually helps the person see it as less threatening, because of the implication of a personality. Unfortunately, it seemed to have no impact whatsoever on Maggie: she hadn't moved a muscle since she entered the room.

As I did my best to make "Daisy" as much like a human as I could, Daisy turned and looked at me, looking severely pissed off. Obviously, I wasn't holding her properly and she was really uncomfortable. As she looked at me, on the outside I smiled brightly at her, speaking to her in a voice that probably sounded like a very strange man talking to his pet puppy: "Hewwo beautifuw, you're such a good girl, aren't you? Aren't you? Yes, you are. You are." In my head I was thinking to myself, What the hell do you think you're looking at?

So, Daisy kept moving about and fidgeting. Eventually, she looked around at me, checked me, turned away, wriggled for a bit and stopped. Then, in a fraction of a second, she span around and bit me right on the hand, just below the thumb. I made an involuntary yelp and dropped the snake back in her box on the table beside me as blood spurted out of my hand.

Meanwhile, Maggie screamed and darted out of the room faster than Usain Bolt and hid in one of the cupboards down the hall.

After a few minutes washing the blood from my hand, I returned and we eventually convinced Maggie to come back in. "It bit you", she said, terrified, to which I replied, "No, she kissed me." But I wasn't convincing. Anyway, after three hours of non-stop work I finally managed to make progress and get Maggie to sit next to and touch the snake. It was one of my toughest jobs ever!

Later that day I phoned Richard to tell him what had happened. After he finished laughing – which included two full minutes of laughter, followed by him recounting the story to whoever was in the room with him – he explained why the snake went so crazy: studio lights agitate snakes a lot and that's why it freaked out. So it wasn't personal. It didn't make me feel any better!

The reality is that when you think about solutions to problems, you can't always guarantee that your plan is going to work. Being able to laugh at the things that don't go so well allows you to focus on what else you can do; because laughter actually helps you think with more flexibility.

Ever noticed that when people laugh they tend to move their bodies back and forth as they do so? Ever noticed that when someone is taking something seriously they tend to frown? Ever notice that when someone is trying to focus on a distant object they also seem to frown? Well, I have a theory about that. When you're trying to see an object in the distance you frown so that you can make the object bigger in your perception. Here's the thing, though: frowning when you're serious also serves to make the problem seem bigger in your mind! On the other hand, if you can laugh at your problems you tend to move back from it, which helps you see it from a distance. Looking at anything from a distance gives you a far better perspective on it.

Often people think that they have to be taken seriously by others. I don't believe so. I believe that you need to be respected by others but not be taken seriously. I want to be able to be playful enough to connect with people in such a way that I can have an impact on them. Most people tend to have a narrow, tunnel-focused view of their problems and they spend time explaining how insurmountable an issue is. The mistakes we make offer us the chance to learn how we can do things differently. Every so often they come back and bite you on the arse . . . or on the thumb!

SECTION 3:
SMARTER EVER AFTER

Rome, 28 May 2010

AS I STEPPED OFF THE PLANE I was exhausted. I mean, five o'clock is a ridiculous time to get up in the morning! I'm sorry, but it is. I had pushed myself out of bed just before the alarm clock screamed at me and I had got ready to go to Italy. After a shower, a last bit of packing and a check-list, I made my way to Dublin Airport.

Italy is a country to which I have travelled many times and I am intimately familiar with – the musical language, the amazing food, the perfectly dressed people.

This time, however, I wasn't going over to teach a seminar but to attend one that Richard was doing. He was teaching a workshop with John LaValle and Alessio Roberti, entitled "The Secrets to Personal Freedom". It was both a workshop in Rome and the official launch of my newest book with Richard and Alessio, *Scelgo la libertà* ("Choose Freedom").

As ever, I was looking forward not only to the training itself but to my conversations with Richard. After he completed the morning session we went for lunch. I got to spend some time with him signing books, before continuing on from where we left off.

In the taxi I had taken to Dublin Airport the radio had been on and there was a discussion of Ireland's bleak future. Since the economic crisis in 2008, the media seemed fixated on who to blame for it. I was tired of all this. I wanted to hear from Richard on this – not on who to blame, but on what was the most useful way of thinking about the recession.

But I had other questions. Having learnt a massive amount the year before from him about the kinds of thoughts that urged him to think of change in a radically different way from others, I was interested in how he tackles the challenges of the modern world.

I myself had found that there was an increasing level of uncertainty in the world and people were struggling with it. With the recession came people out of work, unsure of what to do or what career they would now embark on. Furthermore, the infamous "mid-life crisis" seemed as prevalent as ever, with more and more people I knew going through that stage. The massive amount of information available serves to bombard us all and we feel like we know less than ever about what we're supposed to be living for.

But there was one topic in particular I was most interested in. With the evolution of Facebook and Twitter it is more and more possible for people to reinvent themselves online. This has led to the creation of a huge number of "life experts". It seemed that anyone who had read *The Secret* by Rhonda Byrne was now claiming the throne of the newest self-help guru. It was disturbing and something that I was concerned about.

10. RETHINKING HAPPINESS

IN CONVERSATIONS WITH RICHARD BANDLER I shared my experiences of feeling suicidal when I was young and of being heartbroken later in life. I'm not perfect. But I'm me. What I was beginning to see was a whole host of "experts" pretending that they had no faults, no uncertainty, no self-doubt, no worries about anything. The self-help world experienced a transformation and was now full of perfectly enlightened human beings. As a result of the internet and social-media channels such as Facebook, everyone could suddenly read a few books and became a "coach". They professed the wisdom of positive quotations and marketed themselves by boasting about how many clients they'd "cured" and how happy they were. It was disturbing.

It's not that I didn't believe in making things simple. Quite the opposite, actually: the simplicity of making people happier by helping them to make different movies in their mind and to speak to themselves differently was something I was very familiar with. Not only had I practised and used it on myself but I had found myself teaching people these basic strategies in almost every seminar I taught across the world.

The issue was oversimplification: people would say, "Be happy" and you were supposed to know how. When these concepts were stripped of substance and proclaimed all over the web as being the latest, greatest training or book, it diluted the power of the idea.

What concerned me was the "need" that people seemed to have to show how happy they were. Somewhere, somehow, the idea got out that everyone who was involved in coaching and personal development and the NLP world should just be irritatingly positive and warm to each other. I'm not sure where the notion came from, but it stuck: the NLP and coaching world is full of positive people telling the world how happy they are and saying nice things about others.

Don't get me wrong: I like hearing nice things. It's lovely to hear people saying nice things to you. It makes you feel all warm and fuzzy. But the truth is that what I crave more is "authenticity". What I want is for the other person to be real. I want them to be themselves. In many ways, this book is about teaching you how you can be more fully yourself in a way that makes you far happier with the present and the direction of your life. But we know that telling you what you want to hear won't accomplish this.

I asked Richard about this.

> OF: In speaking about beliefs, one of the things that I've seen quite a lot of in the field of positive thinking / personal development / NLP is this notion that we always need to have a positive attitude, no matter what. But there's a lot of people out there who are almost competing with each other over who's happier, whereas what I've found from my experience with you and NLP is the ability to look cynically at things and laugh at the ridiculousness of the problems that are out there. It gives me a freedom to be able to choose how I feel, rather than try to be positive against all the negative media messages – the ability to laugh at them. People oversimplify, I think.

RB: Well, there's this silly idea floating around out there that, whatever happens to you, you've brought it on yourself. I've had scientologists tell me this. I've had people of various religions tell me this. I've had psychotherapists tell me that if you think negative thoughts, negative things happen to you.

So, basically, they're saying that the reason people get AIDS is because they have a bad belief system and the reason you catch a cold is because you're open to the idea of getting a cold. It's almost the opposite of karma, in the sense that you get what you don't deserve because you're thinking about it, instead of getting what you deserve because you deserve it.

I started out believing that everything works and I don't worry so much about why it works; I just focus on the fact that it does work. So when a client comes in to me I'll try fifty things at the same time. And, you know, whereas a scientist wants to know exactly which thing works, I think humans are infinitely more complex than that. So I think that you have to realise that on Planet Earth stuff happens.

Right now there's a big crisis politically. Some people got shot again in Tucson, Arizona and they're trying to figure out why and the answer to that is actually incredibly complex and incredibly simple: a stupid person had stupid ideas and did something stupid. And that's why these people were killed. When people try to look for cause-and-effect relationships they're going to find what they're looking for. However, there's rarely just one cause.

Whatever the "reason", if radio talk shows hadn't fired people up, this guy probably wouldn't have killed somebody. This guy lived a complex life where billions and billions of bits of information came into him and he probably took some drugs, he probably drank, he may have had stupid friends and stupid parents, he may have read stupid things . . . but even then you could have another person who did all those things and they wouldn't end up shooting somebody.

Oversimplifying the world and believing that you need to always be happy and positive, no matter what, isn't always the smartest approach. Oversimplification is only useful in some contexts. For example, I have studied the language patterns of Milton Erickson, which oversimplified his work. He even said, when he had my book, that it's "an oversimplification of things I do". And, yes, it is: so that we could learn to speak more like Milton Erickson, not so that we could learn to be Milton Erickson or to do the same kind of therapy that Milton did. What he did with people was based on a lifetime of experience.

Nobody could ever recapitulate exactly what I do; nor should they need to, because they're not me. What they need to do is to be able to get whatever skills they can get from me and create their own magical application of those skills. Part of that is believing that what you're doing is going to work, because then you won't get in your own way. But you have to be sceptical where you think that this is all there is. As soon as you start believing in something too much, you get stupid. That's all there is.

If you believe the reason you have problems is because you're open to them, or if you go to a psychiatrist and he teaches you to blame your parents for your problems, that's really an oversimplification. If you're still blaming your parents for all your bad behaviour long after they aren't around, you're not going to take responsibility for it and change what you do. If you change how you feel, it changes how you act and it changes what you do. If you change what you believe, it's a lot easier to change how you feel and change what you do. But all these things interact in an infinitely complex way and the trick is to be able to go in and access these things so that it doesn't depend on everything someone says being true. I don't believe it has to be.

So when people come in and they go, "I grew up this way", "I believe this", "I'm this kind of a person" and, "I've always been unhappy, therefore I'll always be unhappy", the first thing I start doing is making jokes about it. I'm testing what they're doing because I'm sceptical about the fact that someone can predict the future based on the past. If that were true there wouldn't be any progress. It's that simple.

This brought me back to thinking about many of the clients I've had who wanted to know what the cause of their problem was. I've even had clients who believed that they knew and who drew me up a plan of what I was supposed to do to "cure" them. My response always avoided the idea of "cure" and presupposed that, if they already knew the solution, they would have already implemented it.

The proposition here was a significant departure from the vast majority of theories created about problems. What is mostly done is nailing down the specific "cause" and "cure" for any problem. What I was learning was that your beliefs don't necessarily create your problems and that your past problems don't dictate your future problems; but through your beliefs, feelings and actions, you can change things and overcome problems.

OF: What would you say the primary difference between positive thinking, positive hope, positive mental attitude and NLP is?

RB: Well, if your job is to feel good, no matter what, then your behaviour is influenced by what you're perceiving. What you sense directs your behaviour. And, certainly, you can change. Certainly, if you feel something is impossible and therefore you don't try it and you don't do anything, that's a very negative attitude, in my world.

If you positively believe and if you can find a way to do it – even though you haven't yet – then you'll keep trying. To me, that's what a positive attitude is. It doesn't mean that it doesn't piss you off if you don't know how yet, because that's part of what will motivate them. That's what motivates me. When I try something and it doesn't work I get angry. It just pisses me off and I want to know a way to do it. So I start trying to figure out what will work.

OF: So you don't have to be happy all the time?

RB: No. They did an experiment. Psychologists love to torture animals and they hooked up the pleasure centre in a pelican so that if it pecked a red dot it fired off. This released endomorphins into the brain and of course the pelican started pecking the red dot like a pervert masturbating in a XXX booth, you know. Eventually, it died from it. Psychologists draw big theories behind these kinds of experiments: well, pleasure can be too good for you. But, in reality, that's not the smartest insight that you can get from this experiment.

Pleasure and pain are designed to direct your behaviours. Fight and flight are the basic line of defence that was evolutionarily really important. Part of the reason stress is bad for people now is because our fight-flight reaction, instead of firing once a week or once a month, is going on and off all day long.

We're getting wound up because our cellphone is ringing and it's too far away to reach, rather than when a sabre-toothed tiger is biting our head off! You know, since it's not so cut and dried, our nervous system is going back and forth too often for a machine that wasn't built to work that way.

So we need to build cognitive overrides that teach us how to make good judgements so that we don't end up with our bodies stressed out. My last book, *The Secrets of Being Happy*, isn't about feeling the state of joy and bliss constantly: it's about becoming more functional as a human being, aiming your stress so that it propels you in the right direction at a time that's useful, so that you become keen to get things done, rather than fretting over the fact that you haven't. One is useful, one isn't useful.

When you look at successful people it's not that they feel good all the time: it's that their pain and pleasure directs them in useful behaviours. It's not that successful athletes sit around feeling good about themselves all the time and therefore they become the best runner.

I just did an interview with Iwan Thomas, a guy that won a silver medal in the Olympics, who told me that one of the most profound experiences of his life was when he was first tried out for track in college. He ran a race and he didn't win, but he came in, like, third or fourth and all the other guys had gone out and practised every day. But he had hardly practised at all and he said to himself the following sentence: "If I work really hard I might just be able to win this." And it was like a light bulb went off in his head. So every day when he went out he would think that and it wasn't that he was having fun doing it. It wasn't a state of bliss: it's that he set this target. "If I do all of this stuff I might just succeed."

For a number of years now he has held the Commonwealth record in the 400 metres. He said to me that he's surprised nobody beat the record. Part of the reason he beat the record in the first place is that he didn't run against other people. He described to me how he would walk over the course before a race and then he would start running it in real time in his mind, life size. Every time he would get to a corner he would run this stopwatch in his mind along with the movie to figure out what time he would have to be at and learn how to pace himself. So he was running against the clock instead of running against the other people in the race and this meant he didn't always win, but he could always move his time up. What made him a better runner is that he kept moving the clock further and therefore he kept running faster and faster and faster, rather than just running well because of who he was running against.

I remember the first time I worked with another runner. The guy had never won a race, ever. When I asked him how he decides how fast to run, he said, "I like to run about three or four strides behind whoever is leading", which means that if the guy who's leading burns himself out he's going to burn himself out too. And then somebody's going to come from behind and win. Yet there was nothing he did inside his head to judge how fast he could run, based on his own body's ability, his own strength, his own endurance. Everything was off the outside, his performance based on an external measurement of what other people were doing. I remember when he told me that, I thought, this guy needs an imaginary friend more than anyone I'd ever known.

So I got him to make an imaginary runner and run against it. Then he started winning races. You must have some mechanism on the inside that's not based on whether you're positive or not, but whether or not it works positively. You know, if you want to succeed in life you could be happy for absolutely no reason. You can be the pelican whacking and you can peck the red dot until you die. That's not the goal of being a successful human being.

The goal of being a successful human being is having a positive belief that says you can do better and getting a charge from succeeding – and becoming more motivated when you're not succeeding. If you turn your nervous system into a machine that does just that, then you keep finding solutions, overcoming difficulties and doing good – and the worse things get, the better you do. To me, that's what a positive attitude is. A positive attitude isn't always looking at the glass as full and it isn't always about looking at the glass as half full or half empty. It's asking the question, where are all the other glasses?

Richard had once more come out with another Bandlerism that had me laughing out loud.

"Where are all the other glasses?" I repeated it to myself and smiled. There are always more choices in how we decide to look at a situation. Often, people get caught in the black-and-white, "positive vs. negative" approach. The point was simple: if you want to do better you have to base it on what motivates you on the inside and not let it purely be dictated to you by other people.

Propulsion systems
In fact, the modern take on motivation in the field of psychology talks about the difference between "intrinsic motivation" and "extrinsic motivation". Intrinsic motivation is the form of motivation that takes place internally in your mind. The internal sense of pride or happiness in yourself and your values is what dictates how motivated you are. Extrinsic motivation, on the other hand, is when you're motivated by something that comes from the outside, such as money, praise, or physical rewards. Intrinsic motivation has been found to be far more powerful a motivator for people in general.

So, as Richard explained, the basis of creating a more successful life is building the foundations of what propels you on the inside. In many ways, he was talking about something I heard him describe many times before: "propulsion systems". This is a system inside your mind that propels you in a particular direction. The key is that you can use them with positive and negative feelings. So you can turn a negative emotion into a positive one and a positive emotion into something even better.

With this system the more you struggle with something, the more determined it will make you. The more stressed you are, the more relaxed you will become. In this case you turn a negative feeling into a positive one. "The more confident you are, the happier it makes you", for example.

So how does this work? Well, this "system" can be created linguistically or emotionally. A simple language pattern of cause and effect, known as "the more . . . the more" pattern, is a way to create this linguistically. When you tell a person about something you know will happen or is happening you build credibility with them. Then you can say that "the more [this] happens . . . the more [something else] will happen". In this case, "something else" refers to what you want them to experience. In hypnosis the following is often used: "The more you breathe deeply, the more relaxed you will become." Because you've built credibility with the person, they're more likely to believe your suggestion that what happens will cause what you say it will cause.

It's also possible to do this emotionally through anchoring. You can create a positive feeling in the person and anchor it, then get them to recreate a negative feeling and anchor that. You can then fire off the negative anchor so that it starts to create the negative feeling first, then immediately fire off the positive anchor so that it immediately cancels the negative feeling with a positive feeling.

Basically, what you are doing is creating a pattern and linking together one feeling with another. By chaining these feelings you enable the person to go from one feeling immediately to another thereby propelling them in the direction you want them to go in. This can be incredibly useful.

Satisfied that Richard did indeed share my ideas on the "happy-clappy movement", I moved on to discuss how to handle modern-day crises.

11. DECISIONS ON THE FUTURE

I'M GETTING OLDER. Not ridiculously so, but as I write this book I'm in my mid-thirties. When I started writing *Conversations* I was in my mid-twenties. My ten years have certainly been packed with adventure. But now the next big milestone is forty. A few of my friends had gone through a mid-life crisis at about that age. I wondered what was in store for me, although, as I pointed out to them, I've got a full-life crisis. My head is so full of wacky ideas and meandering thoughts about why I'm here and what my purpose on the planet is that I probably wouldn't notice a mid-life crisis if it came along! I wanted to get some thoughts from Richard about this phenomenon.

> OF: There is a theory out there that suggests that many people experience a mid-life crisis. It's when a person gets to the age of forty or so and suddenly feels like they don't know who they are any more. They feel unhappy with their life and they don't know how to proceed. Nothing seems to make them happy, etc., etc.
>
> RB: I don't believe in theories like that. Almost everybody who comes in to me says that they're unhappy, that they don't know who they are and that they don't know where they're going. So whether they're forty and you call it a mid-life crisis, or they're fourteen and you call it a crisis of adolescence, or they just got divorced and you call it a divorce crisis – it's all the same stuff!
>
> You know, people have to go in and pull out the dull, old, crappy images and the whiny stupid voices and take the bad feelings and spin them in an opposite direction and put in shiny new pictures that make them excited. You don't have to get divorced and buy a Corvette Stingray to have an exciting life at the age of fifty. You have to think about what you have and learn to really appreciate what's there and then figure out what you can add to make it even better.
>
> And most of that isn't on the outside: you can buy all the toys in the world and be just as miserable. I have so many clients that are worth a billion dollars or more and they're just miserable sods – especially people who inherit money, or win the lottery. I have a client who won the Lotto and he was still miserable, 340 million later... Miserable, miserable, miserable!
>
> Enjoyment doesn't come from the outside: it comes from your appreciation of the outside. The appreciation is your ability to generate good feelings inside your body and most people are simply not good at it.

"Appreciate what's there and figure out how you can make it even better." I thought about this idea for a second. Was it really this easy? But then, as I considered the alternative, I realised that what makes most crises into crises is the energy and effort we put into them. True, a person may at a certain age feel doubtful about where they're going in life or what they're doing, but it's the dwelling on and the need to answer such questions that lead them into the rabbit hole of uncertainty and despair.

But what about when people are in an uncertainty crisis and don't know what to do? For example, in the modern world, with so many choices, there seems to be an increasing number of people who can't decide on the right job or career.

OF: In terms of career, what would you say to somebody who has no clue what to do with their life in a professional sense?

RB: What you're really talking about is somebody who has been doing something that they don't like and they're fed up! The first thing you have to do is make them realise that what they've done is taken something and made it worse than it actually is.

If people feel that they have to hate something to be able to try something new, then they burn their bridges and they don't expand their horizons. They end up worse than they were, they find themselves out of a job and they still don't know what to do. Instead, you should be able to do what you're doing and enjoy it more and simultaneously start looking around with a view to finding something that you would like to do even better! Read some books, take a night course and watch some useful stuff on TV. You can be searching for the next step as you're doing what you're doing and getting prepared for the next transition.

What people need to do is make a better decision about how to expand and develop one step at a time: "How do I get from here to there?" I have people see themselves where they are now and then project to where they would like to be and then find out what pieces need to fit in between.

Don't say, "If I were there I'd be happy. But I'm here, so I'm miserable." How do you stay happy getting from here to there? You might have sixteen movies on the way to the big movie. Typically, you're going to find something else halfway through that's even better than what you were first aiming at.

You need to love what you do. And I don't just mean at work. You know, if you're going to mow the lawn you should love mowing the lawn. Otherwise you should hire somebody else to mow it who loves doing it. There are some things I really try to get myself to like and I just don't like them! I understand how cars work and I can repair them, but I just don't like doing it, so I don't! I give my car to somebody who likes working on cars. I love driving them, but I don't like working on them. I don't like opening the hood and turning nuts and bolts around.

You can decide which things you're going to like and you can learn to like even the things you don't do so well. I mean, people like the strangest things – people like miniature golf! I grew up in the sixties. I can't imagine anything more terrifying than a golf course with big faces and clowns all over it. That's the stuff of nightmares for me! But when my kids were young and they wanted to do it, rather than dragging myself out and being an asshole, I made myself like it so that I could do it with them. And when they stopped enjoying it I was relieved.

Of course, I knew that what Richard was saying made sense, but I had a problem with it in part. I was lucky enough to be doing what I wanted to do. But I thought about some of my friends, neighbours and family who were struggling and out of work. I wanted to hear from him what suggestions he had for them.

12. THE ANTIDOTE TO THE RECESSION

WE LIVE IN A SOCIETY OF GREAT UNCERTAINTY – one in which we're forced to adapt and change in order to stay afloat. Unpredictability is the order of the day and we find ourselves unsure of where we are and what's next from week to week. The recent financial crisis brought our inevitable vulnerability to the forefront of our minds with a rude awakening. We had placed money at the top of our values and so were treated to a huge economic disaster. Now, money is still important, but we all have less of it. We're in trouble.

In an effort to deal with this issue, many find themselves arguing vehemently against the system, the government, the banks, the policies. In America some want to cut spending and raise taxes; others want to raise spending and cut taxes. Everyone is trying to figure out a way to stay afloat. The truth, however, is that nobody is trying to learn how to swim.

In the world we live in it seems as if we need to fight financial problems with financial solutions. This makes logical sense, but it's fundamentally flawed. I say that because it was financial decisions that led us to where we are today. It was complacency that led us to where we are today. It was greed that led us to where we are today. These are all fundamentally human traits, human habits.

The real solution involves a financial solution, but only after we learn to mentally swim. Swimming in this context requires that we learn how to handle these challenges and difficulties with our attitude, our decisions and our behaviour.

Ireland, my home, was one of the countries most hurt by the recession. Economic turmoil ensued as our recent success became the seed of our most cataclysmic failures. The "Celtic Tiger" economy, as it was known, collapsed mercilessly and we found our very own house of cards come crashing down.

For us it was largely connected to the banking industry and the property development market. Stupid ambition, recklessness and greed served to convince us that utopia would never die and property after property was built and paid for by people who didn't have the money. That and poor government decisions, along with huge mistakes by our banking sector, ensured our rapid and steep decline.

Although it's easy for us to blame the banks, politicians and property developers – indeed, they deserve much of the blame – the reality is that we all contributed to the downfall in our own way. The attitude we allowed ourselves to carry was one of never-ending abundance. We spent like there was no tomorrow and failed to see the potential clouds ahead.

Regardless, as the recession hit, something else hit us just as powerfully: the media. For it was not just our economy that became weakened: our spirit was hit, hard. Newspapers, radio stations and television offered a continuous reminder that we were all as screwed as you could get, except that it could and would, get worse. It seemed to be a bottomless pit of horror we were falling into and the media would describe our downfall with bad news report after bad news report.

OF: Today we seem to be facing more challenging times than ever before. What suggestions do you have for the many people out there who are feeling scared of the future and hopeless because of what is happening?

RB: I would recommend to everybody that they discover a magical button on their channel-changer. It's called an "off" button. And there's another one that says "switch channels". When people start broadcasting how bad things are, you really need to turn off the TV and ask yourself, is it anything different than it was a week ago?

I remember one person I knew who got all of their information about the world from their next-door neighbour, because they didn't go out much and I remember suggesting to them that their next-door neighbour may have been making these things up, totally. And they really needed to find out if there was any basis to it at all, you know – that maybe the stock market hadn't crashed; maybe they just made it up.

Regardless, the fact is that the stock market crashes may or may not affect your life. If you have a big retirement fund full of stocks and somebody has sent you a piece of paper that says they're worth half of what they were, then you have to ask, am I living off the dividends of my stock? Some people are, in which case they have half as much money as they had; or they don't have any money, because they're not getting any dividends.

If you're somebody who isn't going to use your retirement fund for twenty-five years, that may be a really good time to buy a whole bunch of more stocks. The stock market is going to go back up. I know a lot of people who were absolutely morally crushed because the value of their stock had gone down. And when I looked at them and I said, "Ten years from now, will it have gone back up? And will it have gone up more than it has gone down?" And they would look at me and go, "Yes" and I would go, "Then why do you feel bad now?" And they would go, "Well, because my money disappeared." And I would say, "Well, yeah, but it hasn't really disappeared. You have as many shares as you had and it's not influencing the quality of your life now."

There were people who were really hurt by it and the quality of their life went down and they had to figure out whether they had to buy something else that would go up more. It certainly taught a lot of people lessons about being diversified between markets and things. Positive thinking is: "How can I get to a better place? And when do I want to be there too?" Not going, "Oh, my God! The world is ending!" The prophets of doom have been predicting the end of the world since the beginning of it and it's always something new – it's always some new crisis. We get immediate feedback about every horrible thing that happens in the world that we probably wouldn't have known about otherwise. But to feel bad about it isn't going to help.

The question is: How are you going to respond to all this information? What are you going to pay attention to? What actually should influence you? What should you do something about? If you see on TV that they're recalling cars and you own one, then bring it in and get it fixed. But it doesn't mean that you have to get an ulcer about it or something.

OF: What if you lose your job?

RB: If you lose your job, that's the time where you've got to say to yourself, this is the time to get training, to do what you can. You have to go, I really want to get that job back and lose it again and get it back and lose it again.

I think about autoworkers that lost their job but sat around for a year and a half and then the plant hired them back. That's a year and a half where they could have learnt a whole new profession. Especially with computers now, you could learn a whole new profession on the side – one where you'd probably do better and have more job security. As long as you have free time, if they're paying you unemployment benefit you should be getting training in as many professions as possible. In fact, I think most people should think that, whatever job they have, they should have something to fall back on. Somebody like me, I have lots of jobs I do at the same time. If one thing falls apart I'll always have something else going on. I think more people should think about that.

And we've got wonderful things like eBay. You can run a business on the side on eBay. It's always been, you know, whenever unemployment has gone way up there are a lot of people that just go and live on unemployment benefit. They extended unemployment benefit for a year for the United States and there was a big debate over whether they should do it. There's already two years of unemployment – you could live for two years without working – and I can't even imagine going two years without working. It's incomprehensible to me. I would start a business, do all that I could to get a job, do something. But a lot of people don't think outside and they just go, "I'm a plumber", "I'm an autoworker", etc. Their identity is wrapped up in it. And that's a big mistake.

If you lose your job you should not only want another job but you should want the skills to get a job where you become not so dispensable. And certainly there are lots of fields where that's true. There are lots of professions where there are lots of shortages, where you can get the training in less than two years. So whereas someone could stay in unemployment for three years, you could become a nurse in a few years. You can get training in the medical profession. You can learn to be an aircraft mechanic. There are all kinds of things you can learn to do. And, you know, as long as there are cars they are going to break, whether they're electric or whatever.

People who stay current in something can find a way of becoming indispensable and a lot of people who lose their jobs end up starting a small business and it grows into something. I remember two guys that had little income coming in, so they got together and they built this little, tiny computer. One sold his van, the other sold his guitar. I believe the name of that company is called Apple Computer. And when they said they were going to build a computer to use at home, everybody laughed at them and said, "Nobody's going to want a computer." IBM executives who said that are probably asking themselves, how did I miss this? There's always going to be changes in things where, if you're looking for opportunity, you're going to find opportunity.

I met a lot of people who lived on the dole and that was their job and they didn't even think that some day money would run out. In the US, I'm at the bell of the baby boom. There's no way my generation is going to be able to live on social security. There are too many of us compared to the rest of the population. And I don't see my generation planning for that. There is a point

where governments are not going to be able to print more money and pay for everything. I think people need to plan on this and economic crisis is the message. Better plan ahead.
OF: And what do you think are the main points to remember in order to be better with money, to be better at making money, to be better at looking after money?
RB: You have to extend your timeline and you have to look at the future almost like a chess game. It could go really badly, or it could go really well. You don't know. You have to put a little bit aside so you're not living cheque to cheque. I try to do it with my family – trying to teach them to put 10, 15, 20 per cent aside – just keep sticking it somewhere. This means you don't put everything in one place. You don't leave the gold coins out on the counter by a window. When people tell you about great opportunities, you go and investigate. People who invest in companies without having actually been there, I don't get that at all.

I know a lot of people who have lost a lot of money because they read stuff about some investment. I think about Bernard Madoff ripping people off for billions, tens of billions of dollars and I just wonder, because he sent them every month things saying they were worth more. And they went, "Ooh, look how much money I made." That's not really money. That's paper.

I know a guy who invested in a big thing where they built a shopping centre and for two years he was telling me about all this money he was giving and how they were going to make millions and millions of dollars. I remember asking him, "What's the address?"

And he went, "What do you mean, 'What's the address?'!"

It was in another state from where he lived, but I travel a lot and I said, "Well, I'm going to that city. I'd like to see how the project's going."

And he finally dug up the address and sent it to me and when I went out there it was an elementary school – the shopping centre wasn't there. And now we have Google Earth. You can look at anything and see where it is!

If your basis for making a decision is just to trust somebody else's judgement all the time, it's not the way to do it. Sometimes you have to go out and actually look at things. You have to get involved in stuff that has to do with your own life. Especially if you lost your job. You should be asking the question, what kind of job would I really like to do? If they're going to give you unemployment benefit for a year or two years, you could think, well, maybe I'll be back to work three months from now and it won't matter; but maybe what I should do is think what I have to do to get another set of training so that I'd have a job that, maybe, I even enjoy more and make more money.

And yet it requires hard work. You have to read books. You have to go to class. You have to do whatever you have to do. When I was younger, one of my relatives was vice-president of a bank or something – I forget what his job was – and when a merger came along he was out of work. Since he thought of himself as being a bank president and because he had planned on moving up the ladder, he wouldn't get another job. He kept going and applying for a job as vice-president of a bank, but everybody already had vice-presidents. Nobody wanted him. His attitude was, my only other choice would be to go back and be a bank-teller again. And that was unacceptable to him. But with all this management skill and training he had, his brain never wrapped around the idea of going into management, middle management, at some other company that was growing fast and working your way up.

When my daughter started at Starbucks she started out serving coffee, but the company was growing so fast that everybody shot up, so she was in upper management in seven or eight years. If your brain goes out into the future, you need to have a couple of positive possibilities of what you're going to do with your life. And it's better to do that before you're at the end of the road. You're better off doing that as you go along, periodically checking and making sure you have a lot of choices. Then if everything falls apart you have something to back it up with. Too many people depend upon the government to solve their problems and I don't care what country you're in: it's never going to be very good to fall back on a government cheque.

Reflecting on Richard's words, I realised that there were a number of important nuggets in what he was explaining. In a world filled with continuous change it's essential to avoid putting all your eggs in one basket. Indeed, the key is to be strategic and plan for the unexpected, as it may well happen. The learning to take from the recession is to be more careful in how we spend our money.

Richard also made an important point about the fact that the best thing you can do if you lose your job is to get up-skilled. Seventy years ago most people would finish the careers they started when they first got a job. These days, with more possibilities and professions than ever before, there are more opportunities for changing careers after a few years, even if it doesn't always seem like it.

The entrepreneurial revolution of recent times has seen a significant number of people starting their own business. Now, more is possible. The competition is also tougher than ever before, with globalisation and the internet. But to some extent the playing field has been levelled and the proliferation of social-media tools ensures that almost anyone has a chance of competing with the big companies in different markets.

The key is that learning, development and the acquisition of skills are absolutely crucial for your chances of success in the modern world. Of course, it can be tough emotionally to find yourself out of work and it requires a lot of resilience to get through the disappointment of the challenges of the process of finding a job. But as you do so the smartest thing you can do for yourself is to become a learning machine and expand your possibilities.

13. MENTAL SECURITY

WHEN PEOPLE TALK TO ME ABOUT LACK OF MONEY, in many ways what they're actually concerned about is the lack of financial security. The word "security" is a very interesting one. When we talk about security we look at the importance of protecting a nation, person or object against being attacked or harmed in some way. There are security professionals whose job it is to protect and defend something or someone against theft, hurt, or death. Then we have the term "insecurity", which refers to our feeling vulnerable and bad about ourselves, usually in comparison with someone else.

To me, this is the interesting distinction. Being insecure involves you comparing yourself with others in a way that makes you feel not good enough. If we take the phrase "not good enough" and look at it more deeply we can see that in order to be insecure we have to do something inside our head. Often what we have to do is compare ourselves with someone else who we deem to be better than us in some way.

This brings into our awareness the term "better". In the medical model "better" refers to an improvement in health, as in "I feel better". In the performance model "better" refers to an improvement in how you did: "You played better." But in comparisons we make with others we're suggesting that we're better or worse than others. This seems to be quite a natural way of thinking. After all, we spend much of our childhoods (and in the case of professional athletes, much of our lives) competing with others in a sporting sense.

In the business or professional world, again we find ourselves competing in order to make more money, to get a better promotion, to get more customers to buy our products. Competition helps motivate us to achieve more.

So, why do we compete? Well, there's only so much money to spread around. There are only so many potential partners for us. There are only so many positions of power. There are only so many ideal jobs. As a result, we must compete for them and we must be better than others in order to get them.

Unfortunately, there will always be people who are thinner, sexier, smarter, funnier, more entertaining and nicer than us. There will always be people who are better in almost every way we can think of. It's sheer probability. What we need is to change what we refer to when we use the word "better." This can be done by embracing an idea that I call "mental security".

What if you saw yourself differently? What if you imagined hiring a security professional to protect your "self-esteem"? What would they do for you? What would their job be? If you think about it, a normal security professional will look for threats and then take preventive measures to ensure that we're safe from harm.

In *Conversations* I used the term "mental terrorism" to describe how we tend to attack ourselves with our own thoughts. This leads to stress, fear and depression. So the idea proposed here is that you have the ability to employ counter-terrorism strategies against the negative thoughts that might lead to negative feelings or emotions if they are let be.

So, how would you look for threats? Well, the first thing to do is to examine why you're vulnerable. The answer is that you're vulnerable because of your beliefs and thoughts about yourself. For example, if you don't feel good enough at something, you will feel the need to make yourself feel better about it. You will try and let other people know of your successes or your "greatness". Unfortunately, doing this will actually make you look bad, as it will be seen as a sign of insecurity. So your attempt would be like someone buying a lock for their bag after it's been stolen. The crucial thing is to make sure that your bag is protected from the outset.

This means working to make you invulnerable to such threats. So you have to ensure that your self-esteem – how you feel about yourself – is locked up and secure from any negative thoughts or interpretations of any negative experience. You have to be able to feel good about yourself regardless of what happens on the outside, in the world. Your feelings about yourself must remain strong even in the face of criticism or in the face of someone else getting a better job or more money than you.

This is when we return to the word "better". You see, it's okay to see people doing better than you, but what's vital is that you start indexing things. Instead of thinking, they're smarter than me, try thinking, they seem smarter than me in this context. Then ask what you can do in order to become smarter in that area. This completely changes how you feel about yourself, because you stop comparing. Instead, you recognise the difference in results or performance but avoid making it a permanent part of yourself.

Furthermore, it's not about being delusional. If you compare me looks-wise to Brad Pitt, George Clooney or Johnny Depp, it's obviously a tough call! However, the reality is that these guys, some of the most desirable men on the planet, will obviously get more attention than me and will be evaluated by others in a way that trumps me in many areas of life. One great insight I got, though, was when I asked myself the question, if I had to give up everything I have in order to become them, would I do it? When I've asked myself that question the answer is always a resounding No, because I've learnt to like myself and who I am. So, although I might love to have what another person has, I'm secure about who I am.

If someone thinks they're better-looking than me I will accept that's what they think, but I won't allow it to define me. You see, life doesn't work out in such a black-and-white way. There are all kinds of people in all kinds of relationships. There are all kinds of people who are rich and poor. Being intelligent is not necessarily a good predictor for who ends up wealthy, happy, healthy, or successful.

Now, in one or two relationships in the past I've gone through periods when I was insecure. The reason was simple: getting very attached to the other person and allowing myself to worry myself with images of them leaving me for someone else – someone better – made me feel insecure. That was pretty much my strategy. And so I behaved insecurely in response to that feeling. In turn, this made me weaker and it more than likely contributed to the demise of the relationship.

So, accepting yourself as you are is the first step to mental security. You accept how you look, your personality and what you have in your life at present and you learn to be okay with that. You are who you are and you have the face you have and the body you have. You can do something about how you dress and about your body and you can look more attractive by eating right and exercising right and learning to style yourself better. You can have plastic surgery and change parts of your body you don't like. But, more importantly than all that, you need to ensure that you make changes in how you think about yourself. It doesn't matter how much you change how you look if you don't see yourself differently!

You have the personality that you have. You can become more likeable and get on better with others by learning to improve how you communicate. You can learn to get more from life and become more successful by changing how you think and what you do. It's about being honest with where you are and where you want to go.

Once you've accepted yourself, the next step is to do whatever you can to improve in the ways you want to improve – not because you have to but because it gives you more choices. The better you look, the more you learn and the more engaging you are, the more likely you will be to meet more people and to be able to influence more people. The charisma courses I teach are usually about helping people make more of an impact with the people they meet so that they can stand out more and get more out of life.

Fundamentally, however, the key to all this is to change how you think of the word "better". When you're sick, do what you can do to get better. When you're not performing well, perform better. But avoid the trap of being better than other people. Instead, compete to do better and become a student of what those people who do better than you are doing. When dealing with those who seem to be better-looking than you, or richer or more talented, accept that they might have some advantages, but there will always be the flip side of the coin.

The "grass is always greener" concept exists and it manifests itself in society when we look at what someone else has and tell ourselves that we'd prefer their life. From an NLP standpoint this is when we commit an act of generalisation: we ascribe a quality of "betterness" to whoever we compare ourselves with and believe it exists permanently and pervasively.

Security is about protection. Using this metaphor, we need to protect ourselves by exposing our vulnerability and putting in place new ways of thinking that ensure that we can't be harmed by events going wrong or by our own patterns of negative thinking. Our counter-terrorist team is the NLP skills and beliefs that protect us. They are the tools you're learning in this book and will have learnt in *Conversations* and, indeed, in many other NLP books.

Before unleashing your counter-terrorist operatives to tackle negative thoughts that are causing negative feelings, we need to start from a more secure and fundamental place. This means focusing on doing better than others and even being better . . . but not being better than others. It means reminding yourself that life isn't necessarily fair. You need to just get over this and do the best you can with whatever you've got. It means accepting you as you are and you as you can be and feeling the security that comes with knowing that, regardless of what anyone else says, you are okay. It's all a matter of what you focus on. Then you will experience true mental security.

What I learnt from Richard that afternoon in Ireland has stayed with me until the present day. His insights on happiness and crises enlightened me about a new way of thinking. Of course, I already knew that it was necessary to focus on the solution to a problem and not on the problem itself and I encouraged others to do the same. But what really clicked for me was the importance of getting back to basics and learning to make the inside of your mind a brilliant place to live in. It means not buying into media brainwashing about what is happening and, at the same time, seeing whatever challenges you face as an opportunity to learn and to grow. It means seeing the choices you do have and ensuring that you're actively and regularly engaging in actions that help you feel good.

Bit by bit, the jigsaw was coming together for me. Hope continued to occur as a theme in what Richard said. The decision to believe in what works for you, the decision to think in the most useful way possible, the decision to believe in a better future full of opportunities – all this without evidence that things definitely will be better. You believe that they will be anyway.

It was already quite an adventure. The next time I'd see Richard would be in his house in the United States and it's there that we would continue our conversations.

14. RANDOM RAMBLINGS: THE RACE TO INTELLIGENCE

SOMETIMES HAVING A BRAIN ISN'T EASY. Every second, we're stimulated by millions of pieces of information. The information we absorb through our senses is interpreted as we extract meaning and understanding from it. What we extract depends on the sorts of beliefs we already have, mixed with context, mixed with what happens. We're continuously trying to predict what will happen next so that we can be in the best position possible to make our lives better and happier.

There are many suggestions about the best way to work with your mind. In the early days of therapy, psychoanalysis was regarded as the best approach. Going into your past and finding the deep, dark, lurking issues that were repressed in your mind was presented as the ultimate key to happiness. In the middle of the twentieth century, with psychoanalysis increasingly discredited, along came behaviourism. This approach suggested that humans were in many ways just like animals. We could be conditioned. Two ways of conditioning us cropped up: "classical conditioning" and "operant conditioning".

Classical conditioning refers to the process invented by Ivan Pavlov of pairing the sound of a bell with "food time" for dogs, mentioned earlier by Richard (p. 16). This led to an understanding that, to produce a behavioural change in humans, you could associate pain with a negative behaviour, thereby making that behaviour less likely to occur. Similarly, you could associate pleasure with a positive behaviour, thereby making that behaviour more likely to occur.

The term operant conditioning was coined by the famous behaviourist B.F. Skinner. It refers to behaviour that is changed by its consequences, that is, by what happens after the behaviour takes place. So when you give someone a reward for engaging in a behaviour, they're more likely to engage in it; and when you punish someone for engaging in a behaviour, they're less likely to engage in it.

Both types of conditioning focused on retraining new forms of behaviour. Although they produced some good results, there were problems with them. One in particular was the lack of understanding of what actually goes on in the mind. The word "mind" itself is actually a metaphor and only describes a model of how we think; it isn't an actual, physical "thing".

Cognitive psychology bridged that gap and so began a war between cognitivists and behaviourists. I say "war", but it was really just a continuous debate during which study after study attempted to outdo the opposing hypothesis by proving it invalid. After a few years a new form of therapy, cognitive behavioural therapy, was invented. This involved using the best insights from both approaches to help the client to change.

NLP came along just before cognitive behavioural therapy was formed, in the late 1970s. In many ways it offered a cognitive behavioural approach, as it too looked at thoughts and behaviours and suggested strategies for helping people change in both these areas.

The principal difference between therapy done using NLP and that done with cognitive behavioural therapy is that NLP looks at how we think, rather than just focusing on what we think. While there seems to be much in common, in NLP we look at the qualities of the mental images a person makes and at the inner voice they use to talk to themselves.

In positive psychology, a relatively new branch of psychology, there is a focus on the concept of happiness and on what makes people happy. One great insight referred to often by cognitive behavioural therapists, as well as by positive psychologists, is the difference between optimists and pessimists. Optimists believe that when something goes wrong it's transient ("It's just happening now"), situational ("It's just this situation") and specific ("It's just in this particular case"). Pessimists, on the other hand, believe that when something goes wrong it's personal ("It always happens to me"), pervasive ("Everything is messed up") and permanent ("It will always be like this").

What I always found interesting is that many of the recent findings in the areas of positive psychology, cognitive psychology, neurology and behavioural psychology actually support the kind of ideas that were expressed when NLP was jointly founded.

The problem many people have is that, just like the need to be right, they have a need to seem intelligent. Now, this becomes a problem, as people often act the way they do because they believe it will make them look smarter. As well as the "happy-clappy" trap I talked about earlier, there is also the "I'm the smartest NLPer on the planet" trap. These are the trainers, authors and bloggers who use an extensive array of jargonic annunciations (yes, I made that expression up!) about the "true nature" of NLP or its related concepts. They attack everyone else who isn't in their gang, claiming that mass stupidity and ignorance are rife.

They may be on the money occasionally, but such an elitist viewpoint is itself stupid. To me, the smartest people are those who do the smartest things, not those who just say the smartest things. Pretty much anyone can read tons of books and claim elevated status as a result. I used to see something similar in university: professors positioning themselves as smarter than each other, new research papers claiming the throne of intellectual superiority. It reminded me of the American presidential election debates, where both candidates do their very best to bullshit the viewers into buying their promises.

It's the same issue: it's about what other people think, not about who you are. To me, real intelligence and being smart comes down to what you decide to do. If what you say has a positive effect on others it can classify as smart as well. But the decision to make things inaccessible to the everyday person serves very few.

Being smart is seeing things from different points of view. It's seeing that you're often wrong and that that's okay. It's seeing that you're right when you think in a more useful way and that you can do something about how you feel and how you act. It's in realising that you get to determine your own brain chemistry if you work on your thoughts. It's in understanding that the smartest approach is often a simple one, but one that requires action. That's intelligence to me.

SECTION 4: MAGICAL LANGUAGE

Richard's House, United States, 2011–2014

WHEN I FIRST OPENED AN NLP practitioner manual, at my very first practitioner training, I turned the page and saw terminology such as "lost performative", "selectional restrictional violations", "nominalisations" and "subordinate clauses of time." It scared the bejaysus out of me! I was already well versed in hypnosis and hypnotherapy, yet these words were alien to me. I didn't realise that NLP was a foreign language.

In the end, I saw that it wasn't. As I continued learning NLP, what fascinated me most was the area of language. I became transfixed by how language worked. When Richard would tell stories and use hypnosis, when he'd have conversations with clients, I always noticed that he had a way of using the right word at the right time in the right sequence in order to get the right response from the right person in the right context.

Now I was back in America and had just arrived at Richard's house. It was quite late, but he was still up. It was great seeing him again. It was also nice being somewhere that wasn't covered in snow. I had managed to fly out of JFK Airport in New York only an hour before they closed it because of storms that had just arrived there. Richard showed me around his place. I'd missed him since he was no longer living in Ireland. After chatting for a while we sat down in his office and began the conversations again. My next topic of interest was language.

Language is an important part of the technology of NLP. "Linguistic" is, after all, NLP's middle name. Indeed, the very first NLP book, *The Structure of Magic*, was ultimately about how language can be used to implement change. The first two formal models of NLP, the "meta-model" and the "milton model", initially seemed inaccessible to the lay reader, as they were based on some of the linguistic theories of Noam Chomsky. To help myself understand them in depth, in my master's thesis in applied psychology I dealt with Chomsky's seminal theories on transformational grammar in analysing language. I had by now developed a good understanding of them both, but I wanted to hear more about them from Richard.

It's evident that beliefs are absolutely critical in helping people change. Beliefs are affected by language; words are the very foundation of change. This was my opportunity to explore with Richard some of the intricacies of how he thought about and used language and beliefs. First, though, let's look at the key models involved.

Get the point!

The look!

Richard on time out

The flyer for Richard's talk with Robert Anton Wilson in London in 1997

15. ASSAULTING LINGUISTICS

NOW, I'VE GOT A SIMPLE BRAIN and I think in a very simple way. Throughout my master's thesis, in which I was confronted with the necessity of using the relevant jargon to explain my ideas, I concentrated on understanding the concepts at a simple level first, before translating it back into the complicated terminology. Although this took more time, it meant that I felt more comfortable about my understanding in the long run.

The problem is that I will often be accused of oversimplification in how I describe things. When it comes to linguistics in NLP, I see two main types: those who teach the language patterns by rote, because they don't fully understand them perfectly and those who feel the need to overcomplicate by inventing new models and derivatives that don't seem to add any practical benefit.

Besides Richard, there are only a handful of trainers I've found who are really good at explaining the language models simply. Among them are John and Kathleen LaValle. I found myself getting a lot from their explanations. I never felt the need to do what some trainers do and go into transformational grammar and the complexities of general semantics in depth in order to teach people how to use language to effect change.

I spent eight years in university and came out with first-class honours in my chosen subject, applied psychology. I'm not a genius or a rocket scientist, but I can understand the academic treatment of the various NLP models. However, I've never found anything while looking through the various theories that helped me to do better change work with people or to become a more effective communicator. What I saw was a form of intellectual masturbation, with various authors trying to outsmart each other with even more grandiose and complex propositions about what the most "accurate" way to study language was.

At a seminar I was taking part in I once heard a well-known trainer from the very early days say, "I have no beliefs."

I put up my hand and said, "That's a belief."

His reply was, "No, it's not: it's a fact."

To which my response was: "You believe it's a fact."

He then condescendingly said, "You obviously don't know the difference between beliefs and facts."

I replied, "You believe that I don't know the difference between beliefs and facts."

Now, I wasn't just trying to be annoying (although I was certainly accomplishing that feat). What I was trying to do was to point out something simple about what all this language stuff is about. We have beliefs and they limit us or empower us. The kind of beliefs we have will determine what becomes possible for us.

I'm going to attempt to give you some clarity about how all this works. (Of course, if you want a fuller explanation – but not necessarily a more practical or useful one – you can always go deeper into studying transformational grammar and the updates and critiques of Chomsky's work.)

The patterns of language that evolved into the original meta-model and milton model primarily came from studying Fritz Perls, Virginia Satir and Milton Erickson and how they used language. They were coded by the application of transformational grammar and that's where the many terms come from.

Meta-model

Transformational grammar, proposed by Chomsky, suggests that every sentence has two structures: a deep structure and a surface structure. The idea is that there is a structure common to all languages, known as a deep structure. This refers to the semantic relationships between concepts – what we know commonly as the meanings of sentences. The surface structure refers to the expression of those meanings. The surface structure of statements is connected to the deep structure by a process known as "transformation". Although Chomsky has moved on and no longer uses this model, for our purposes it is a simple and convenient way of explaining how the meta model works. What we're most interested in is the fact that, during this process, information gets deleted, distorted and generalised.

So when a person has an experience it is filtered through their senses and through the beliefs and meaning they already have for that experience. Everything they could already say, think and feel about that experience is the deeper meaning. What they actually conclude from this experience – the belief that arises – can be seen to appear as a surface-structure belief.

The meta-model questions have three main functions: specifying information, clarifying information and, by doing both of these things, opening up a model of the world. In other words, by asking questions that get a person to be more specific and clear, you help move them towards their deep-structure meaning. The questions serve to challenge their limiting beliefs, helping them to recognise the deletions, distortions and generalisations present in their language.

For instance, "nominalisation" in language is when you turn a process into a noun. For example, a client of mine once came in and said, "Panic attacks follow me everywhere." Panic attacks are referred to here as if they're "things", when panic is actually a process. My response to her was: "Close the door and make sure they can't get in. Dammit! What am I going to do now that they know where I work?"

This ridiculous response pointed out the silliness of what she was presupposing in her statement: that panic attacks could "follow" her. The reality is that she found herself "panicking" – it was something she did. By challenging that nominalisation, I got her to see the distortion present in her language and enabled her to think about it differently so that she could have more control. After all, you have the ability to change what you're doing but not necessarily what "stalks" you!

Other NLP devices, such as "sleight of mouth" patterns, also help challenge such beliefs by verbally reframing them in such a way that the belief sounds less logical, with a less solid foundation. I give an example of a sleight of mouth pattern under "The Language of change" (p. 96). The whole aim of these questions and patterns is to make language more accurate and to create doubt in the limiting beliefs a person might have.

Milton model

There needs to be a way of helping people adopt more useful beliefs and ways of thinking. You can do this through the "milton model", named after Milton Erickson. In some ways this acts as the opposite of the meta-model. It's designed to be "artfully vague" and actually uses deletions, distortions and generalisation strategically to build beliefs.

For example, politicians will often say something like this: "Vote for me and I promise that we will find fair and adequate solutions to the challenges we face. I promise that we will move forwards, not backwards and create the kind of future that our children will be proud of."

Sometimes they'll be even sneakier: "Specifically, what will I do? Well . . . I will ensure that we make continuous progress in implementing the policies which most benefit those in need and I will endeavour to unearth those policies that are wasting the taxpayer's money."

"Huh? What now?" I hear you say. Exactly! Even when they promise to be more specific they're just as vague. But guess what? It's nearly impossible to argue with them or attack them for what they've said. As we hear it, we go inside our mind and we interpret it in a particular way, because the ambiguity forces us to find our own meaning in what they're saying.

The milton model also provides us with a set of language patterns that allows us to be more persuasive indirectly. By using truisms and artfully vague language, you can build credibility in yourself as a source and in the argument you're making. You can also give someone suggestions that are outside their conscious awareness. For example, instead of trying to get someone to hire you by telling them directly ("Hire me now!"), you could put it like this: "As you're considering whether or not to *hire me now*, I'm wondering whether or not you *believe in giving me this position*, as I feel that if you *do, it will be the right decision*."

By embedding the suggestion inside the larger sentence and using downward inflection when you make the suggestion, you make it more likely that the person will take it on unconsciously and automatically. The downward inflection makes it more likely that they'll take it on board, as it marks it out as an actual suggestion. While not giving them any specific logical reason why you're the right person for the job, you're making it more likely that they will feel unconsciously that you are the right person.

In the course of the study of the use of hypnotic language it was discovered that a person could be given a suggestion in a number of indirect ways. Possibly the most interesting part of hypnotic language is the use of presuppositions to embed assumptions in a person's mind indirectly.

Presuppositions are a part of almost every sentence you can think of. You presuppose something when you assume it to be true within a sentence. So instead of saying, "This is a really great phone", which is a direct statement that could be challenged, you can say, "One of the reasons this phone is so great is that. . ." You are using a number of presuppositions in the sentence to make the statement seem as much of a "given" as possible. The layering of a number of presuppositions in a sentence is called "stacking". This makes it harder and harder for the other person to challenge the truth of what you assume in your presuppositions. Richard has used hypnosis and also implemented post-hypnotic suggestion, the process of giving a person a suggestion that they would then carry out in a waking state.

Logical influence
Creating a logical argument is one way of convincing people of your ideas. However, you don't necessarily need to use logic accurately. Indeed, there is a host of what are known as "logical fallacies" that enable you to argue in way that seems logical but that isn't in fact based on an effective rationale. Actually, this doesn't matter, as we're not interested in being logical *per se*. Rather, we're interested in getting someone to believe something more useful. Rhetoric tends to be used by speakers using such fallacies to persuade and influence.

Also important is the influence of general semantics and the work of Alfred Korzybski in *Science and Sanity*. Korzybski's famous dictum "The map is not the territory" became one of the fundamental principles of NLP and in many ways it explains the principal idea quite clearly. Korzybski's suggestion is that we create abstractions from our experiences by means of the words we use and the more we do so, the less accurate we become in our descriptions. We abstract at a sensory level when we describe what we're experiencing in terms of our five senses.

Also, the more we use language, the more we find ourselves talking about less and less directly verifiable and measurable objects. The issue is that the less we accurately index our experiences, the more likely we are to stray from sanity and develop generalisations that limit us. For example, most of us will have a similar enough understanding of a chair, but when we talk about such concepts as love, morality, happiness and inner peace, the more room there is for misinterpretation and distortion.

At about the same time, Benjamin Lee Whorf and Edward Sapir put forward the idea of "linguistic relativism", which states that how we use language affects how we conceptualise the world. More recently, Steven Pinker and George Lakoff have discussed the importance of metaphors in shaping how we experience particular concepts.

The work of NLP therefore seems to be nicely aligned with a number of prominent theories. The way you use language has an impact on how you experience your world. Change how you use words and you will change how you think about that world.

Now, the difference between our approach and that of some of those theories is that we aren't interested in always making language more accurate and we're not interested in understanding the mechanics in depth. Instead, we're interested in finding ways of using language to help people get out of the mental prisons they put themselves in. (and that's an obvious metaphor). We do this either by abstracting, when it's useful, or by becoming more accurate, when that's useful.

The meta-model, the sleight of mouth patterns, the milton model, the use of logic – all these serve to uncover the inaccuracies of our limiting beliefs and help us to construct more useful beliefs that serve and empower us. That's the bottom line.

Teaching a seminar on Influence in Lithuania

With Brian Colbert during our workshop in Bangkok, Thailand

"Yeah just make that cheque out to…" Backstage after speaking at an event with Sir Richard Branson

Richard in concert!

Fun times with Richard

16. LOVING WORDS

✦

IN JULY 2010 I took a trip to Iran. While I was there, huge demonstrations were taking place in the centre of Tehran, only a few streets from where I was staying. Late one afternoon I went wandering and I kept walking and walking. There was a particular restaurant I wanted to visit. I wrote the name on a piece of paper, but after an hour's walking I still hadn't found the place, so I hailed a taxi and gave the driver the piece of paper. After a half-hour drive I found myself in the far side of the city. I realised that the driver had got confused: we were nowhere near the restaurant.

I got out and looked around me. It was evident that I stood out like a sore thumb. Then something occurred to me that made my heart sink: I hadn't brought the address of my hotel with me. Even worse, I couldn't remember its name. So there I was, stuck a thirty-minute drive from my hotel, with no idea which direction it was in. It was a sticky summer's evening and I was feeling hotter than ever as I looked around me for signs that might help. I couldn't recognise any whatsoever.

For the next couple of hours I walked around trying to find someone who spoke English. In that particular part of Tehran anyone I approached seemed to have no word of it. Taxi drivers wouldn't stop for me. Many people eyed me with suspicion. It was approaching ten o'clock. I started wondering what I was going to do, how I was going to be able to direct someone to where I was staying.

Speedy and I on the streets of Tehran

Eventually, I decided that desperate times called for desperate measures. I began flagging down passing cars. Finally a motorbike stopped next to me. The driver, a kid who looked about sixteen, asked, "Where go?" I responded that I didn't know but that it was near where the demonstrations were taking place. He didn't understand at first, so I began to act out scenes of people demonstrating. I became the demonstrators as I made the kind of sound I'd heard them make. He looked at me quizzically, but finally he seemed to get it. He offered me a seat on the back and said he would take me there.

I had no idea if he understood a word I'd said. But it was the first opportunity of a lift that I'd had in two hours and it was getting darker every minute. I jumped on. The kid started to speed off and within minutes we found ourselves on a huge highway. Traffic in Iran is ridiculous. It makes India look like the safest place to drive! I hung on for dear life as my driver (Speedy Gonzales!) weaved in between huge cars and lorries going 80 to 90 miles an hour. My elbows just about touched two rear-view mirrors at one stage; we were that close to both cars. It was scary as hell.

After about forty minutes of this we came to a stop. I got off the bike feeling completely tense and exhausted. The good news was that he had understood me: I recognised where we stopped as being right next to where the demonstrations took place. I simply followed the road I had taken earlier and I arrived back at the hotel in a few minutes.

In travelling the globe, I've often had to rely on my ability to communicate a message non-verbally or, at the very least, by using body language as well as words. The language barrier can cause challenges in communication between cultures and lead to misunderstandings galore. What I've also found, however, is that there is another language barrier that exists within each language. This barrier is in the form of the variety of ways in which your problems can be "read into" by "experts". Often, therapists and coaches find themselves making assumptions based on the theories they've learnt, rather than paying attention to the patient or client in front of them.

What I've discovered is that there is a lot you can understand by thinking in a more simple manner. I wanted to start by asking Richard about one of the mistakes many people make upon becoming "experts" on language: they find themselves drawing conclusions and working under assumptions that aren't necessarily accurate.

> OF: What I've found is that, on stage or in your videos, clients may talk at length about an issue they're experiencing. Some go deeper into the problems and start getting technical, but you can cut through all the noise and focus in on the real problem, even if the person hasn't mentioned it directly. What do you pay attention to in order to be able to find the real issue?
>
> RB: Well, I'm a simple person. I'm looking for what's simply going on. I realise that problems don't exist in the world: they exist in the world of ideas. One person's happiness is another's misery. It may seem ridiculous, but that's how it is!
>
> So here's a woman who wanted to be a ballerina, but the thought of dancing on a stage in front of people almost made her have a panic attack. And it wasn't just dancing: it was everything. She put so much stress behind everything she set up that it was invariably easier not to do anything rather than attempt to do the things she really wanted to do.
>
> She had no problem imagining herself dancing in a room with no people, but put the audience there and it was panic stations. But it's still the same room. It's still the same dancing. Whether you dance alone in your bedroom

or you dance in front of five hundred people, it isn't profoundly different. You can get paid for one and not the other – that's the big difference!

You see, she couldn't conceive of it because she'd built in the panic attack. The attack had nothing to do with dancing, it had nothing to do with being in front of an audience and it had everything to do with the pictures in her head.

When I asked her about it, I simplified it. I said, "Look, if you went into your living-room and there was a disgusting picture on the wall that made you want to vomit every time you looked at it, would you leave it there?" Of course, she said, "No." I then asked her why would she then leave a horrible mental picture of herself failing and making a fool of herself in front of people, of getting so nervous that you throw up. "How can you leave the picture in your head? What's the difference?"

Now, my ability to simplify these things stems from my firm belief that they are simple. If you believe that there are deep psychological underpinnings to things, then you have to make everything complicated and I don't believe that things are complicated. Human beings, by their nature, are uncomplicated.

Make a picture, get nervous – and if you're not nervous enough, talk to yourself enough until you are! – check to see if you're feeling bad and keep spinning it up, obsessing on it and pretty soon you will be feeling awful!

I can hypnotise people and put them into exactly the same states that they put themselves into. The main difference is that it's harder for me to hypnotise them than it is for them to do it to themselves. But if we can both hypnotise them and make them feel miserable, why can't we do it and make them feel wonderful?

I brought a gentleman onto the stage at a seminar the other day, put him into a deep trance, had him go and find an overwhelming sense of joy – one amazingly wonderful memory – and turn it way up to the point where he felt giddy and then to look at where he felt there were failings in his life. In his case, it was approaching his boss: every time he got around his boss he got so nervous that he couldn't function. There are a lot of people who just can't act normal when they're nervous, which makes sense when you think about it. But if you're going to be nervous around the person who can give you a pay increase, more authority at work, a promotion, etc. . . . Every time you have hopes for your future you need to get around the person who can help it happen – your boss can! So you need to stop acting like a babbling idiot!

Most guys do it when they ask someone on a date. They're not being the person they really are! They go into their mind and make themselves feel so nervous and uncomfortable that they're hopping from foot to foot, acting like the Hunchback of Notre Dame instead of the person they really are. And there isn't any difference between asking someone on a date and asking your mother for a Coca-Cola.

But if it's different in your head you create a situation where you hang horrible pictures in your mind. You make lousy music in your head and unpleasant feelings. Then, of course, you start to believe that that's who you are. But it's not who you are: it's what you're doing. The techniques that I use with people teach them how to control their mind – how to control the voices, the pictures and the feelings – so that they can have the right pictures, feelings and voices at the right time.

To me, that's a very simple thing. Whether it has to do with a high-performance executive, a schizophrenic, or a girl who wants to dance ballet, it's all the same thing. If you have the right thoughts in the right place, it's easy. If you don't, it's really hard!

So much of the field of NLP had become complicated. There were advanced models in this area and that area. One of the things I really appreciated about Richard was his desire to make everything as simple as possible in order to help people change.

Now, I'm familiar with the complicated terminology and the ever-growing list of models. But I knew that what Richard was saying made absolute sense. Having worked with thousands and thousands of people in a therapeutic context, I realised that I was always looking for the simplest way to do things. There will be critics who have their own theories about the correct approach, but typically it involves helping the other person by paying attention to them as fully as possible. Sometimes a theory can get in the way, as it encourages the therapist to see things that aren't necessarily there.

One of the things I've learnt to do is to pay really close attention to the words a person uses and how they use them. This can be a blessing or a curse and, indeed, it has proven to be both for me.

It's a blessing in that it helps me truly understand what the person actually thinks and the real issue behind whatever they're saying the problem is. It allows me to understand far more about them than most people would know, because I've learnt to extract a massive amount of information deductively, which is available from a small amount of data.

It's a curse in my personal life in that my attention to language allows me to know when someone isn't being fully truthful with me. A lack of congruence in the words used, an irregular word choice, a way of explaining something – all these give clues to what the person is saying and trying to say. Being too aware of what's going on around you can sometimes be troubling. After all, the relationships you have with loved ones aren't always black and white. We don't live in a world where everyone always tells the truth. But sometimes it's nice to pretend we do.

All in all, the ability to notice more of what's going on around you can help you massively in becoming more effective at persuasion. The more you know about how someone is thinking, the more options you have in influencing their thinking.

Given the possibilities for how NLP can be applied, it makes sense that one of its most popular applications is based on persuasion. Marketing experts, advertisers, politicians, salespeople and business leaders alike have been taught the skills of NLP in order to help them become better in the areas of persuasion and influence.

You'll be hard pressed to find a book on persuasion that doesn't refer to or make use of some of the patterns that have been discovered in the field of NLP. Richard had written a brilliant book, *Persuasion Engineering*, with his co-trainer John LaValle. In it you can learn a fascinating model of and approach to sales and influence based on Richard's latest work, as well as find out about John's own experience and developments in the area. I wanted to know more about how Richard thought about persuasion.

> OF: You've met a lot of very persuasive people. In your book with John you both presented a great model of persuading people. What do you think the first thing to keep in mind is when someone wants to become more persuasive?

Magical Languages

RB: Well, there are different kinds of persuasion. To begin with, there are people who are intimidating and that's one kind of persuasion. I have no interest in that. There are lawyers who convince people of things, but the way in which they're persuading people I don't approve of. A lot of them do it just by lying. I've seen it in court atrocities committed under the legal system, but that's how it's kind of designed.

Not everything people are persuaded to do is something I would agree with in terms of persuasion, but you can't underestimate its effectiveness. I mean, John F. Kennedy was an incredibly persuasive person. I don't happen to agree with most of what he said – he wasn't my kind of politician – but he was incredibly persuasive in his use of language. Obama, again, very persuasive – at least he was. We'll see how it works out for him in the future.

To me, there's a difference in the art of persuasion in different contexts. When I look at great public speakers, I see a lot of people who are incredibly persuasive. You look at salesmen. A guy like Ben Feldman sold millions of dollars' worth of life insurance face-to-face – a much more difficult sale than getting somebody whooped up in a political convention. To me, all of these things fall into different categories and they're really different skills. Being a great salesman is a different task than being a great politician or a great public speaker. You kind of have to sort those things out.

In the explanation of the different approaches on this topic, you will find that four areas of persuasion are examined: (1) the source of the message, which relates to you when you're trying to be persuasive; (2) the message itself, which is how you deliver the message you're trying to get others to believe or act on; (3) the medium, which refers to the channel or context in which you're presenting the message; and (4) the audience, your understanding of how your audience thinks about how you present the message.

Here, Richard was talking about the medium of your message. The idea is that you have to consider the various contexts you find yourself in if you wish to influence another person effectively. Often people don't do that. They just run into the situation with a bunch of theories or beliefs they want to tell people about. Being more strategic in your efforts at persuading or influencing other people is critical.

Of course, focusing on how you make the other person feel is very important and, depending on the context, there are a number of ways to do this. The more you can present your message in a way that engages all their senses and the more you can deliver that message so that all aspects of it are congruent, the more impact you will have on their feelings. This means ensuring that your body language, facial expression, words and tone of voice all match.

Sometimes you might adjust the environment for the person as best you can in order to influence them in some way. For example, I remember going to a spa in Taiwan. The walls were a soothing sky-blue colour and had pictures of sunsets and beautiful scenery on them. Very relaxing music was being played in every room, each of which was scented with lovely aromas. Before and after the massage you were given a cup of a particularly minty version of green tea. The whole experience was congruently telling you to become as relaxed as possible.

Of course, an essential ingredient in changing someone's mind is the strategic use of language, in particular what I call the "language of change".

17. THE LANGUAGE OF CHANGE

"SO, WHO HERE HAS GOT SOMETHING they're certain about that doesn't make them feel good?" I asked the audience. I was back in India. It was December 2005 and I was teaching NLP language skills to a couple of hundred people. I was about to demonstrate some more patterns of the meta-model.

A man put up his hand and I waited for the microphone to reach him.

He stood up and said, "The Indian secret service are in this room and they're spying on me."

I smiled. I thought he was kidding. Then I looked in his eyes. He was not. At first, while not 100 per cent certain yet of whether the secret service were watching, I got the audience to ask him questions and challenge his beliefs.

"Who says?" someone shouted out.

"I say. I know my father has hired them", he responded.

"Hired who?" another person shouted out.

"The agents. They're over there."

The two men he pointed to really did look the least like secret service agents of anyone in the room. Both were in their late sixties and one had missing teeth.

"How do you know?" he was asked.

"They're wearing transmitters", the man responded.

Someone else suggested, "Why don't you search them for transmitters so we'll know if they're spies."

The man replied disdainfully, "I already know it and you won't find anything. They're really good at this."

This was a good answer. The audience was stumped. There was no real way to challenge his beliefs effectively. As I listened to his responses, becoming certain that he was in fact convinced of what he was saying, I knew I needed to help in some way.

You see, the excellent skills of the meta-model won't always convince the person you're talking to that they're wrong if they're already really convinced of what they believe. In the case of schizophrenia you aren't just trying to get them to doubt a limiting belief: you're dealing with strongly held convictions based on a distorted experience that sometimes includes hallucinations. Being told that the devil is speaking to you is difficult to doubt when you actually believe you're hearing his voice. So, with this in mind, it often comes down to helping the person adjust their beliefs around the problematic belief.

For example, in *Conversations* I related a story of a client I worked with who believed he was a superhero and I suggested that he needed to practise his skills one step at a time. I taught him a number of NLP skills, such as creating the kind of feelings he wanted and being more effective at influencing others and I referred to these skills as particular powers. I also suggested that he needed to avoid letting people know about his superpowers, as most superheroes have an *alter ego*. This helped him think about his belief in a much more useful way. So instead of challenging the direct belief ("I'm a superhero"), in which he had invested a lot of time, I was challenging the beliefs about what that means.

I learnt this from Richard's work with schizophrenics. When Richard met "Andy", who believed that people were coming out of the television set and into his living-room, he suggested changing the channel to the Playboy Channel. This ingenious suggestion was a great example of what helped Andy to take more control over his experiences. Instead of saying, "The people aren't coming out of the TV", Richard focused on helping Andy handle this experience, because it was distressing him so much.

While many psychiatrists have tried for years to talk patients out of their beliefs by arguing with the illogical nature of such beliefs, Richard had a different approach. Giving Andy the idea that he could handle the hallucinations he was experiencing enabled him to feel more in control of his life. By helping my client who believed he was a superhero to see everyday, useful skills as superpowers and having him not tell other people, I ensured that he was able to function more effectively in the real world. Accepting the Indian seminar participant's belief that the secret service were following him enabled him to think about this paranoid delusion in a way that made him feel much better about it. The key is that we were helping them feel differently.

People don't just grow out of hallucinating and creating delusions and simply come back to reality. In fact, there's a contextual issue here as well: if you see a man on the street explaining that he was talking to God, chances are you may perceive him as a mental case. On the other hand, if you're in a church and a man on the altar speaks as if he's talking to God, in the here and now, chances are you'll accept that this is exactly what he's doing! One way to look at problems is that we all suffer from our own delusions and hallucinations; the key is to help ourselves by creating the kind of delusions and hallucinations that make us feel really good and help us achieve our goals.

Richard's philosophy has always been that if the person isn't in touch with reality, then change reality. The key to doing this conversationally lies in your ability to use language effectively and to switch your frame of reference in terms of what you're focusing on.

To me, this is one of the primary distinctions between how Richard thinks about the change process and how so many others, even NLPers, do. Many people see the change as being in the technique or the process. Richard works on enabling the person to set their life in a whole new direction by thinking differently. He does this, in no small part, in the way he uses language.

Whether it be through a sophisticated language pattern or through hypnosis by means of post-hypnotic suggestion, Richard has an in-depth understanding of the nature of language and change. I wanted to get a better insight into how he thought about words and the impact of words on a person's mind.

> OF: One of the aspects of NLP is linguistics. What do you think are the biggest insights that you have come up with, with regard to how language works?
>
> RB: When you look at the work of Noam Chomsky, he had a model of transformational linguistics and the mathematical structure of human language, but, in and of itself, all it did was describe how the unconscious mind processes information and how we speak language. It didn't tell you anything about processing it differently. He talked about deep structure and surface structure, but what was missing was what you can do to help people.
>
> So the meta-model made it possible to understand, when somebody says something to you, that it's a nominalisation or a deletion, as Chomsky would describe it. Psychotherapists, without realising it, were asking about those things. Virginia Satir would ask a question like "What stops you?" but she

didn't realise she was challenging a linguistic limitation that Chomsky had outlined.

Between John Grinder and myself, we figured out that the process "orientated" questions. However, the questions were still aimed in the right direction; questions were aimed to get people to describe their model of the world so that you could understand it.

It's a two-way street. You're not only identifying the language that comes out of a person: you're feeding language back in. And it's the interactions of those two things that can alter somebody's state and change the way they process information. It isn't speaking differently that gets you to think differently. Instead of continually making the same pictures, or talking to themselves in the same voices so that they end up with the same feelings, you can tell people how to actually make a new feeling. For example, so that they can get in the elevator and not be terrified.

A lot of those techniques came through asking people who'd gotten over problems how they did it and what came out of the trial and error were ways to get people to think differently. For example, if a client came in to me and they had a phobia of washing their hands, I was going to constantly send them back to the sink until they weren't terrified. And, you know, I wasn't going to do it a week from Thursday. I was going to do it over and over and over again while they were sitting there.

And when I made that decision my goal was to fix the clock. Anything and especially hypnosis, was used to learn to hypnotise somebody and, in a deep trance, have them do something. You can even get somebody who's terrified to speak to an audience – you can hypnotise them and get them to go up and sing with abandonment, without hesitation and then you bring them out of the trance and they can't even turn and face the audience. This means the brain is capable of it!

So the clock is only broken if it's wound one way, but when you wind it this way the same clock works perfectly. So the clock ain't broken: it's just not being wound. Then everything gets easier. Then you're not looking for how it's broken: you're looking for how to open up the rest of the brain so that it will do what it would do if you put him in trance.

I remember a person who had some weird disorder, a psychiatric disorder, where if he saw a toilet he felt like he couldn't pee. But if he knew that there was no toilet available he felt like he absolutely had to pee. I put him in a trance and I set it up so that when I touched him on the right knee he felt like he had to pee and if I touched him on the left knee he felt like he couldn't pee. Overwhelmingly. And then it didn't matter if there was a toilet. I could open the bathroom door and see the toilet and I'd touch his right knee and he would feel like he absolutely had to pee and I'd close the door.

I could switch him back and forth. I could use post-hypnotic suggestion. There was a group of psychotherapists and a couple of psychiatrists sitting there. Everybody thought it was funny. Even the guy thought it was funny, because he knew I was just screwing with him. (I even told him I was screwing with him.) I brought him out of trance and I said, "There's no bathroom in this house" and he would go, "Oh, my God, I absolutely have to pee" and I would touch him on the knee and he would go, "I can't pee" and I'd touch him on the other knee and he goes, "I have to pee" and I'd touch him again – "I have to", "I can't", "I have to". And everybody in the room would laugh and the psychiatrist says to me, "Well, as long as you have him hypnotised you can do this. But is he going to have to touch himself on the knee?" I said, "No, you missed the big picture."

The big picture is that it doesn't have anything to do with the toilet. The big picture is that it doesn't have anything to do with me hypnotising him. The big picture isn't about his touching his knee or not. The big picture is that this is completely out of control. So all you have to do is build a control mechanism so that none of this matters ever again. I said the important part is to make this unimportant. I asked this guy how long he's been going to therapy about this problem and how much time during the course of a day he spends worrying about whether there's a toilet or not. And it was overwhelming. He said, "It's from the time I wake up until the time I get to bed. And it been like this for fifteen years."

Me, I'm a mathematician. I start calculating out. Okay, so if he's awake sixteen hours a day, start adding this up – it's just a massive amount of time. I go, "When this problem's gone, what are you going to do with yourself?"

He looked at me and he goes, "Maybe I could try and be happy." He'd had no experience of being happy.

"Where are you going to start?"

He goes, "I just sat here and laughed at my problem. That's the first time I've ever done that."

And I said, "Yeah and you're never going to be able to stop. Every time you see a toilet you're going to have to laugh a little bit and go, 'You used to be the boss of me. But no more'."

In an hour and a half I can take something that overwhelms his life and turn it into a joke.

Then the psychiatrist was asking me, "Well, where do you think this started?"

And I go, "It doesn't matter. It's over."

And he goes, "But, you know, we didn't get to the real root of the problem."

And I said, "Well, actually we did. The root of the problem is that it's a problem."

The root is that it's a problem. It's not a problem now, so it doesn't have a root. It's over. The clock ticks. He is just like you and me. He can go in and pee and when he's not peeing he doesn't have to think about whether there's a toilet or not. Isn't that what it's about? It doesn't matter. The reason that it was built up in his head is that he had giant pictures in his head of the toilet and him needing to go. It doesn't matter where the pictures came from. They're not there any more.

What I was getting from what Richard was explaining was that the idea of using language successfully to help people change was a two-way process. The work he did involved understanding the difference between the way his clients thought about their problems and the way other people thought about the very same things. It was just a case of challenging what they thought and replacing it with a new and more useful way of thinking.

Richard was able to identify the limiting beliefs and thoughts behind the problem. In this case the idea of needing to go to the toilet was the issue. When Richard fed powerful suggestions back in, it changed the way his client experienced the problem.

For instance, Richard used a great example of the "propulsion systems" change discussed earlier. The suggestion he gave the client was that every time he saw a toilet he was to laugh and think to himself, you used to be the boss of me, but no more. Richard created a cause-and-effect belief for his client.

Giving someone who feels compelled to feel a certain way the ability to think about it differently lets them have a choice in how they deal with it. One of the biggest problems was that many therapeutic approaches focused on trying to uncover the "cause" of problems, rather than exploring how they worked to limit the person. Richard continued by explaining the problem with this cause-effect mentality when it's oriented in the wrong direction.

> RB: It's like asking a question: If a tree falls down in a forest and nobody's there, does it make a sound? Well, people call it a sound. If you put a tape recorder there and a person listens to it you can sneak up on the forest. It makes sound waves. That's a different question: Is a sound wave a sound unless somebody hears it?
>
> Those are philosophical questions. I started out majoring in philosophy – that isn't a part of philosophy that interested me. What interested me was the part of philosophy that did symbolic logic, where you could take meaning and quantify it and qualify it. And you could figure out whether things are logical. But it doesn't tell you if they're true or not.
>
> The fact that things can make sense and be untrue is an important part of understanding the world. The most important thing I learnt from philosophy was that you can have a logical thing – "All green cats are on the table" – then you know that if there's a cat on the table, therefore it must be green. It sounds logical, but it isn't. It isn't logical and it isn't true. And the fact that you can say something is always the case doesn't mean that the example even fits it. There are counter-examples of everything in the universe. It's just the nature of the universe.
>
> Everything achieves paradox at some point in time, including this sentence. Understanding these things allows you to concentrate on processing information differently. So the big understanding about language is to understand that language isn't about truth: language is about logic. It represents what we're thinking. It represents unconscious processing, but it doesn't mean it has to stay unconscious, or that it has to stay that way. Building validity in your thinking means that you can believe things that are totally valid yet absolutely untrue and it can be useful.
>
> That's the importance of building hope. I'm probably not right about the fact that every client that comes in can be helped quickly. But, so far, I have pretty much been. Believing that is a useful belief. It doesn't do me any good to search for the ones that can't be helped.

Magical Languages

Where Richard differs fundamentally from many others is in his emphasis on the importance of what is useful, rather than on what is true. Linguistically, the ability to help people believe in ideas that help them grow and learn and change is what makes the difference. As we learnt earlier, in the need to feel certain we find ourselves believing in many different ideas. Since all of them can't be true, the question is no longer "What is true?" but rather "What do you define as being true?" Truth is defined by our beliefs.

The reality is that there are quite a few logical fallacies in how we think about things. It's on those fallacies that many beliefs are built and with them many beliefs are changed. Some of the patterns in NLP use the same fallacies that the questions of the meta-model help to challenge. It manages this because it's focused not on what is "true" but on what expands the possibilities of what a person can do.

18. PARADOXES AND PRESUPPOSITIONS

IN ORDER TO UNDERSTAND more about how beliefs change through language, I wanted to get an example from Richard.

> OF: Could you give a simple example of a particular language pattern that changes beliefs powerfully?
>
> RB: Well, the times I'd seen Virginia [Satir], she'd get someone to change the way they'd thought about something. A lot of it had to do with finding counter-examples to things that they absolutely believed. When they go, "Nobody could like me", Virginia would look them straight in the eye and go, "I like you". It collapses it. I once worked with a woman who said to me, "I can't say No to anyone" and I'd go, "Tell me No" and she was stuck. One way or the other, she had to! It's a double bind.

A "double bind" is when you give someone an idea that paradoxically contradicts one of their beliefs and traps them into finding a fault inherent in the belief itself. For example, one day, when I was helping out on one of Richard's seminars in Edinburgh, a man came up to me and said, "I have a problem I need your help with. I feel I'm really stupid and that's getting in my way. Richard told me to talk to you."

I was hoping Richard didn't mean "You think *you're* stupid? Wait till you talk to Owen!" Anyway, as we chatted, I pointed something out to him.

"Here's the thing: Is it smart to do what's useful?"

"Yes", he replied.

"Is it stupid to do what's not useful?"

Again, he agreed.

"Is it useful to believe you're smart?" I asked.

"Yes."

"Is it useful to believe you're stupid?"

"No."

"So", I pointed out, "if you believe you're smart you will be smart, because it's useful and therefore a smart thing to do. On the other hand, if you believe you're stupid you will be stupid, because that isn't useful and is therefore a stupid thing to do."

After spending a moment or two considering what I'd just said, he smiled and nodded his head slowly. "I never thought about it in that way before."

Later, in the workshop, he came to me and thanked me, because from that point on he kept reminding himself of this new way of thinking and it changed how he felt completely.

This is a simple example, but it points to just how powerful junko logic can be. It's also an example of the sleight of mouth pattern known as "apply to self", in which you use the belief to destroy itself paradoxically. This successfully reframes the way the person is thinking and therefore challenges it effectively. It's one of the coolest and most powerful patterns in language for helping to produce change. Richard continued to discuss, in more depth, how he thought about language.

RB: When you look at guys who did heuristics – guys like Gregory Bateson and people who studied meaning in the sense of how it functioned systematically, instead of studying semantics – they'd looked at language in terms of general semantics.

My generation is the first generation that could benefit from Chomsky and Bateson and all of these people. Had they not been there I wouldn't have the understandings I had in order to develop what I did. I guess that's why in some introductory philosophy books you study Gregory Bateson's work and then you study me and Grinder, because they still consider part of what we did to be about philosophy.

It's the philosophy of language. Building a meta-model was an important step, but it was an important step logically. But it couldn't have existed if these other people hadn't done the things that they did. You have to read Wittgenstein, you have to read Bertrand Russell, you have to read all these people, to understand, to have the foundation to draw the conclusions we did.

The conclusions we drew were very powerful and we built the linguistic model – the meta-model – which was where we took a model of language and used it to ask questions in order to gain more information. It wasn't about the truth of the information. The information told us what the model of the world was. It told us what was in it and what wasn't in it. So it told us how to blur the lines. And the specific techniques which became what I consider some of the powerful parts of NLP were when you introduce the notion of submodalities and you start explicitly rearranging thought patterns and learning patterns. What we used to call "strategies" in the old days evolved into something much more important. We understood how the submodalities influenced the way people thought and how they structured their beliefs.

John and I spent a lot of time in science libraries perusing journals, finding out what they knew about how the brain worked. When John and I parted ways I didn't believe that we were close to discovering what was the powerful part of what we were developing. It's a lot of work to figure this kind of stuff out and to keep experimenting with a lot of people to try different things, to find out rapid ways of getting people to shift their model of the world so that they can engage in new behaviours.

To me, I think the important thing that I'm doing now by interviewing successful people and asking them how they do it is to get the emphasis away from repair and towards what it really should be: optimising human beings. I think NLP offers the greatest tool to people in the educational system, especially early childhood education and teaching people how to do art, music, math, reading, writing and how to run all the machines we're going to have to live with.

For years, when I heard Richard talk about NLP I had heard him explain it as an "educational tool". Now the reason he emphasised this point was becoming more and more apparent. The focus he had now was based on the idea that we can learn quicker and better once we understand how we think. This also accounted for the evolution of Design Human Engineering®. Richard strove to help people become better, not in the medical sense of the word but in the developmental sense.

It was becoming clear that in order to truly master language we must watch it in action and practise using it. Indeed, I had found that myself. Ever since the earliest days, when I became familiar with the meta-model and the milton model, I used these ideas over and over again until they became second nature to me.

One of the parts I practised in particular was that of presuppositions, the language pattern in which you could assume something in your language while talking about something else. By assuming it, you make it more likely that the other person will just accept what you're saying. It's extremely powerful.

OF: First of all, one of the things that I did want to ask you about – something I've seen you talk about and use so many times – is presuppositions, presupposing that change is going to take place and using presuppositions in language to enable the person's mind to be directed. Where did you first become aware of the power of using presuppositions? One time you said that, referring back to having a particular problem, presupposing that all the rest of the time you're going to be over the problem is one of the most powerful uses of language.

RB: Of course, you go back to predicate calculus. Examining the presuppositions of an argument is a big part of doing logic. When we were using mathematics back in the old days to programme computers, we had to transform English into zeros and ones. Even if you're designing an accounting programme on a computer you can't accept presuppositions the way people do in normal language; you have to ask everything twice.

Of course, I could hear the presuppositions that people were using – not just the clients but also people like Virginia [Satir]. Virginia would always say to people that she would reconstruct something in their history and say, "Now, when you go back and look at it with new eyes. . ." My brain would go, wow, that's a pretty big presupposition. But people just accepted it and did it. Also, there are presuppositions in hypnotic trance work. When you say, "Now, as you relax. . ." that pretty much presupposes that you're relaxing!

I was trained to hear logic when it was spoken. As soon as I recognised how it was being used I wanted to maximise it. The most elegant instructions to somebody are always the best; the more presuppositions you stack makes it more likely that things are going to go your way. That's why one of my favourite things is "I want you to try in vain to run that memory." Well, it presupposes that they're not going to be able to do it. When you say, "Once in a while when you look back and you have some of those old feelings", it presupposes that most of the time they won't! And saying, "The difficulty in recalling an old problem is that it doesn't matter any more" – so when you now look back, don't worry about the difficulty you have, because, even though you know you had a problem, it won't feel like you any more.

Something like that stacks so many presuppositions inside just a few sentences that they're different. If you don't believe that they're different, how are they going to believe they're different? And the inverse is true. I've seen people who were really changing and I've seen people absolutely screwed up, because you say things like "Each time in the future when you're as terrified as you were. . ." which presupposes that they're going to be terrified again.

"I know it's hard for you to live with this depression" presupposes they have depression. That whole idea in psychology is that you had to accept your problems in order to get over them. And accept yourself the way you are. Once you accept you're a depressive, then you won't be a depressive, or some such nonsense!

In reality, the way that they're talking to people convinces them unconsciously, due to how they process language unconsciously. For me, I want to maximise everything; I wanted to use every technique that makes it easier for people. Of course, stacking presuppositions is the icing on the cake. Sitting in my office years ago, all I had in it was one trance chair and a piano stool. There was absolutely nothing else in the room. I wanted no distractions. There was nothing, not even a picture on the wall. The old trance chair was from the Victorian age and the legs were really low, so the people would feel really small. The room itself was very small and it had really high ceilings. At the far end of the room there were three steps that went up into the bathroom. If I began to speak to people like a child when they sat there, they would begin to feel like a child, because it was all miniature in the corner.

And I remember once this person came in and – more as a joke than anything – I sat them down and I towered over them, looking down sternly like a disapproving parent. And I said, "Now, you have a really terrible problem, don't you?" Just one tag question. And I said, "What was it?"

And he looked up at me completely dumbfounded and he said, "I can't remember."

And I said, "Hurry up, or you'll never get it back."

And the guy got into a panic and asked me if he could use the phone to call his psychiatrist to find out why he came there.

So I called the psychiatrist and I asked him why he sent that guy to me.

And the psychiatrist goes, "What did you do to him, Bandler? He's been struggling with the same issue in therapy for six years."

I put my hand over the phone and I looked at the client and I said, "Sir, your psychiatrist claims you've been in therapy for the past six years dealing with the same problem – what was it? Try as hard as you can to remember."

Of course, when you say, "Try to close the door", it implies that people won't be able to do it.

He was blank and he couldn't do it.

Finally the psychiatrist said, "Let me talk to him."

And I said, "Not a chance – if you talk to him he'll remember!"

And he said, "If he represses the problem it'll come out somewhere else."

And I said, "Isn't that a good thing?"

And the psychiatrist goes, "No."

So I hung up the phone and I sat down and I said, "You've repressed this problem." I said, "You know what happens when you repress a problem? It comes out somewhere else."

So I put him into a deep trance. And I told him, as soon as he remembers this problem he's not going to be able to feel the way he felt, because it's been adequately repressed. Of course, the way it's going to come out is in a burst of happiness that he'll feel for no reason and he'll start to enjoy life and feel free. And any mention of this in the past is going to cause uncontrollable giggling, to the point where he might even be embarrassed. That should be enough.

To me, it's important to understand how to stack presuppositions. It's not just one sentence that does it: it's the continual onslaught of the logic saying that it's an undeniable reality that your problems are in the past and they've been replaced by good things in your future.

Almost every technique I use is designed around that. You get rid of the bad stuff and you amplify the good stuff. Where you have bad pictures you push them away and where you have good pictures you bring them close. See yourself in bad pictures, but step inside of good pictures. I mean, it's a simple logic – I'm a simple guy, really! Although the technology I've created appears vast and, for some people, appears complicated, it's not if you don't think about it as being complicated.

Although I was already quite skilled in using NLP language patterns, understanding Richard's thoughts on it all got me thinking. I considered the various patterns I found most useful. Perhaps my favourite of all was the category of presuppositions. To me, they are a really good way of building more useful beliefs for people to believe in. Language kept coming down to the same thing: you challenged limiting beliefs and built resourceful beliefs. That was basically it, what it was all about: helping people change what was real for them so they could think in smarter ways.

At the seminar in India the troubled man looked up at me questioningly as the audience went silent. My response was immediate. "That's so cool. You're so lucky."

"What do you mean?" he replied.

"Secret service agents following you everywhere, that's fantastic. You're just like the president."

He looked at me quizzically.

"That means you're far safer than most people out there, because you have these two guys watching your back." I smiled down at him and waited.

After a few seconds his anxious expression turned into a relaxed smile. "I never thought about it like that", he said.

I continued, "Most people have to pay for that kind of service. You get it for free. Nice." It was a change of reality.

The simplicity and sophistication of language, together with how it can be used to produce change, was something I was becoming ever more fascinated with.

At Richard's house it was getting late and it was time to sleep. The following day I would continue with my questions about communication. But this time I would ask about some of the most important relationships we have.

19. RANDOM RAMBLINGS: WORD-WEAVING

IF WE WANTED TO GIVE YOU some kind of hypnotic experience while you read the words on these pages, what would we do? Would we ask you to focus on every word and hear our voices reading them to you in your mind? Would we ask you to slow down . . . and speak . . . in a relaxing tone of voice . . . to yourself? Would we ask you . . . to use a very soft and smooth way . . . to help you become more comfortable?

You see . . . the language we've talked about here . . . discusses a number of different things . . . and if you follow each sentence . . . it's possible for you to realise . . . that the aim of what follows . . . is to help you understand . . . that in order for you . . . to become more effective with language . . . there is a way . . . a powerful way . . . of recognising that we all build beliefs . . . inside our mind . . . and we do so from . . . when we're very small . . . because when you grow up . . . you learn language . . . you learn how to speak . . . you hear your parents say . . . "Mama" and "Dada" . . . and you learn to repeat these words . . . you learn to create associations . . . Now, those associations help you to understand . . . that there are names to our experiences . . . labels we can use . . . words that tell us about the world . . . about our experiences . . . like this experience . . . of reading these words . . . knowing that they have meaning . . . and wondering what meaning you can take from them . . . because inside language lies the truth . . . and when you think about thinking . . . and feel what you're feeling . . . you can just notice . . . that noticing you're relaxed . . . helps you feel even better . . . and feeling better . . . comes from knowing that something is changing . . . because since you were very small . . . you learnt so many things . . . and now is the time . . . your time . . . to realise . . . through your real eyes . . . that the real lies . . . you told yourself . . . were the limitations you had . . . the limits of what you could do . . . of who you could be . . . because none of those limits matter . . . Never mind . . . instead, you can start . . . inside your mind . . . to begin to believe . . . like you did when you were young . . . in magic and magical places . . . places where you can be all you want . . . where you can feel all you want . . . where you can do all you want . . . in abandon . . . in freedom . . . allowing your spirit to roam free . . . because that's what it's all about . . . it's about taking a trance . . . taking a chance . . . to move forward in time . . . to where you remember to forget what isn't needed any more . . . and to start to remember what is needed . . . The ability you have . . . that you've always had . . . to make changes . . . in how you speak . . . in how you communicate . . . so you find the right words . . . at the right time . . . in the right context . . . for the right person . . . so that you can . . . powerfully . . . and easily . . . become more persuasive . . . influence others more easily . . . because as you imagine . . . yourself in the future . . . using language brilliantly . . . saying what you need to . . . in the most effective way . . . getting the best responses . . . winning over opinions . . . and you can know this . . . gets easier . . . as you notice so much more . . . and you learn so much more . . . so you keep getting better . . . How on the pages . . . between the front of this book . . . and the back of this book . . . you can discover . . . from this cover to that cover . . . you can find yourself . . . and find yourself experiencing . . . a tranceformation . . . as you form a new trance to change . . . and you let go . . . of what you don't need . . . so you can simply be . . . fully and completely . . . in the present . . . in this moment . . . which you'll never have again . . . because it's the now . . . and will always be the now . . . but never again . . . instead . . . you can see . . . the newness of the now . . . that you get to choose . . . you get to decide . . . that it's time . . . to shine . . . to rewind . . . to a time . . . where all was fine . . . remembering a time . . . where you felt you were flying . . . feeling like you could soar . . . a great future in store . . . feeling good more and more . . . as you begin to ignore . . . bad feelings and explore . . . how to open the door . . . feeling good but now for . . . no reason whatsoever . . . as you become smarter and cleverer . . . so you use your brain for a change . . . No more pain but in range . . . of a beautiful life . . . free from stress and strife . . . so you can feel like you desire . . . as you ignite the fire . . . of the strength inside you . . . the power that helps you break through . . . so you can open the filter of what you perceive . . . take more control of what you believe . . . and as you start to widen the funnel . . . you see the delight at the end of the tunnel . . . and you return to the page that you're reading right now . . . so you can look forward to your future thinking . . . Oh . . . Cool . . . Wow!

If we did want to give you an experience of what hypnosis is like, we'd probably say something like that. But we won't. Again.

SECTION 5:
LOVING RELATIONSHIPS

Richard's House, United States, 2011 – 2014

THE NEXT MORNING I woke up and went downstairs. Richard was already up. After spending a few days with him, I planned to embark on a journey through Central America. It was on my list and I would have much to learn from the experience.

In the book *Conversations with Richard Bandler* we talked about love and heartbreak, loneliness and friendship. But there was more I was curious about. I wanted to ask him questions I had been asked quite a lot recently regarding relationships, parenting and nurturing talent and potential. I had given my own answers, but I wanted Richard's input.

In that book I also discussed my first real experience of heartbreak. I openly and honestly explained how that break-up affected me and I discussed the perspective I got from it. That relationship lasted only a short time. It stung mostly because it was my first real break-up. I learnt a number of lessons, which I recounted. I pretty much had it all figured out. Quite a few people commented that they found that section really helpful as they went through their own break-up.

At Christmas in 2008, five years after this first experience of heartbreak, I met someone else I fell hard and fast for. This time it was different. We spent most of our free time together. We travelled the world together. We moved in together. We opened our hearts to each other. It was destiny. Finally.

20. THE SOUND OF A BROKEN HEART

Have you ever heard the sound of a broken heart? I sat in my car in the driveway and stared at the black rings around my eyes in the rear-view mirror. I hadn't slept. It was the middle of the morning and there was no-one around. All was quiet. I thought about what had happened. I thought about what it meant. I thought about her. We had been together for a year and a half. We had broken up a couple of months ago, but I still had hope. Now it was all dashed. One phone call. The last phone call. It was over. She was in love with someone else.

I kept staring at myself in the mirror, secretly wondering how I could get through this. Again. And then I broke down. As I did so, I began to notice the sound I was making. It wasn't whimpering sniffles I heard: it was the sound of raw agony. Full, emotion-filled agony. In the sounds I made, I could actually feel the pain. This torture continued even after the tears dried.

I've experienced my fair share of pain. I've cracked two discs and pinched a nerve in the back of my neck that shot bolts of agony down my arm. I've had second-degree burns on the majority of both my legs and ended up in a wheelchair. I've broken bones and been in plenty of accidents. I know what it's like to be overcome with a sharp sensation that beats the life out of you. But, in that car, this was pure hell.

Like every experience, this one changed me – quite dramatically. It was like a reset button for my heart. The romantic, idealistic Owen was given a rude awakening into the real world. This time there would be no return to the naïve, blindly optimistic Owen. He was gone. He had moved on.

In the beginning, as in every full-on relationship, it was magical. Addictive, intense, exhilarating – the concoction of chemicals you're promised in every love song and every romantic movie. A soulmate connection. An incredible closeness. Romance, love, all the frills. At the beginning it's exciting and you feel like a legend, like you can do no wrong. The final piece of the jigsaw has fallen into place.

But somewhere along the line I found myself acting like someone I didn't like. I became a walkover: one-dimensional, intense, insecure, stressed, depressed. That wasn't me and yet it was how I was. I invested all my happiness and self-worth into the relationship and I lost myself. I forgot who I was, what I was and my purpose in life. Meanwhile, I taught courses on NLP and happiness. I was still confident in myself in all the other aspects of my life, but I lived in fear whenever I thought of the relationship. So attached was I to her that I was petrified about it ending. I tried my best to control things and fix things, to keep her happy . . . and that just made things worse.

Being good at what I do requires me to read people really well and I could read her. The problem was that what I read terrified me. I was too perceptive for my own good. My instinct told me one thing; my heart badly wanted me to be wrong. The subtext of our conversations was giving me the message. But my inner mind had its fingers in its ears and was screaming, *"Lalalala, I can't hear you!"*

Ultimately, she met someone else, fell out of love and we broke up. We were both to blame. But, given how some things had transpired towards the end, I felt betrayed. I was hurt. Rejected. Devastated. Someone so close to me. A part of me. It felt like I had got it all wrong. It was all a lie. The promise of it all was broken. You wait your whole life to meet that person. And then it's not it. They're not who they're supposed to be. Pain. Alone. Again.

For months afterwards I stayed angry with my ex. Coaches I know preached that I needed to "let go" and "move on" and "forgive and forget". Like it was a light switch. But it wasn't. They scolded me for harbouring any sort of resentment, as if it was a weakness and as if simply giving up the negative feelings was an easy choice. They regaled me with stories of their own terrible heartbreak and how they instantly forgave and let go, how they were completely fine within a few days or weeks. This oversimplification was way off the mark.

Now I was that author, that speaker, that NLP guy who was supposed to be in control of my feelings. I was informed that my reputation was in danger of being harmed. That's when I came to my next conclusion: I don't give a shit about what I'm supposed to be or supposed to feel. I'm not prepared to pretend to everyone that everything is perfect. I didn't in *Conversations* or any other past books, I don't in the seminars I teach and I won't in my life either. That conclusion felt liberating.

After *Conversations* was published I heard from a lot of people who were surprised and delighted by my raw honesty when it came to my account of falling in love and experiencing heartbreak. The fact that I was so open about my weaknesses, stupidity and suffering wasn't expected. Why? Because we live in a society where we give utmost importance to how others see us. How can I command respect if I show my weak side? But the ability to be vulnerable and show your weakness is actually your greatest strength.

Many people spend their lives living to impress others. They seek to be liked and loved. They seek to be looked up to. But life is like love: it's only when you can let yourself be vulnerable that you can truly get the most from the experience.

I mention all this to explain some of the most important lessons I have ever learnt, which came from this experience. You see, getting rejected and being left for someone else actually made me far stronger than ever, far more confident than ever, far more secure than ever. There were three key lessons I learnt from this experience.

Firstly, I learnt never again to allow my life to become one-dimensional. If you invest all your money in one stock, any problems with that stock can jeopardise your entire financial future. It's like what Richard spoke about earlier in regard to looking for a job or how to handle money: if you invest all your energy, time and happiness in one area of your life – whether it be your relationship or your career – you risk jeopardising your entire future happiness.

Secondly, I've learnt that I'm far stronger than I gave myself credit for. I realised that I could face one of my worst fears and not only survive but also go through it better and stronger than ever before. I became strong because I didn't have any other choice. I'm 100 per cent certain that the times you found yourself at your strongest were when you most needed to be. That's when you start to find out about your character.

Thirdly, I've learnt that relationships are like learning to swim: the more tension you use, the more fearful you are of drowning; and the more you try to grab onto the water, the more likely you are to struggle. In terms of relationships, the more you try and control everything perfectly, the more you are causing those things to die. Love prospers when you embrace it. Not when you grab on tightly to it.

I still have memories. Memories filled with love. Memories filled with anger. Memories of nostalgia and regret, bliss and devastation. The most important thing is what you decide to learn from those memories. I thought I had it all figured out, but I didn't. Now I've figured out that I don't have it all figured out and that's what I believe will make the difference.

When someone dies you have only your memories of the time you spent with them. In a relationship, you hold a particular perception of your partner in your mind. When a relationship dies, the person appears differently to you as this perception changes. You no longer think of them the same way. Therefore, all you have left of that time together are the memories of what it was like. You move on and the memory feels different.

The sound of a broken heart comes in many forms. It can come in the silence between partners who know it's over. It can come with the words "There's someone else" or "I'm not in love with you any more." It can come in an intolerance-filled sigh or an exasperated grunt. It can come in faint whimpering or agonising wailing.

The sound of a broken heart is a horrible, horrible one to hear. But we need to hear at the same time that things will be okay. Everything will be okay again. At the time, it feels like it won't. The key is to look back and remember the good times for what they were. Just like you can never have your childhood back, you can never have that relationship back. Indeed, since you're different now, it just wouldn't be the same. As Richard so beautifully put it, "The best thing about the past is that it's over." Once again that saying helped me massively.

The trick is to focus on the next wonderful experience you can create. You have to ask yourself different questions. Is there someone you can connect with even more deeply? Someone that you can grow with and develop a strong bond with? Someone you like as well as love and who likes as well as loves you? Someone who is different, special, unique – who gets you like you get them? Someone who will for ever be loyal, kind, generous and thoughtful and treat you as you treat them? Someone who is your dream partner, born to be with you and you to be with them?

Maybe there is; maybe there isn't. For me, maybe I've met her, or maybe she walked right by. Maybe I haven't met her yet. The beauty of life is the adventure you go on in order to find the answer to questions such as these. So, come what may, it's about looking forward, not backwards and remembering the lessons that the past has taught you so that it can be invested in a better future. And instead of wasting time asking questions, it's about continuing to move forward, no matter what, not about absorbing yourself in what's gone by.

After all, looking forward is what keeps you going when times are tough. It's what enables you to overcome the challenges that can sometimes knock you. As my good friend Robert Orr says, "Life is tough. You have to be tougher." That means digging deep when you find yourself hurt, lost and alone. It means believing in yourself and knowing that everything is going to be okay.

I've met some incredible women. Many are my friends to this day. I'm blessed to have been lucky enough to connect with some of the most beautiful souls you could ever imagine. The future is bright and I expect even more amazing people will continue to come into my life.

For months after the break-up I found myself on autopilot. I got into a routine of getting as fit as I could and working as much as I could. I went through a phase when little bothered me and little excited me. My emotions had been deadened – exhausted, really. It's like there's only a certain amount of emotional pain you can experience. It's difficult to embrace the tough times and such horrible feelings. Heartbreak can wind you and leave you floored. But the key is to be there for yourself, to remind yourself of your value, of all you have going in your life. And to remember that lifting the biggest weights builds the strongest muscles. As you look forward to the bright possibilities of the future, the adventure of the unknown, you are able to experience hope. It enables you to remember that "this too shall pass". It enables you to become stronger. Once more, the answer lies in the idea of hope.

21. THE ULTIMATE RELATIONSHIP

NOW, IF YOU'VE READ *Conversations* you're probably getting tired of my break-up stories. It would be nice to have a sweet, romantic story to tell you at this point. But, alas, I have something else I need to talk to you about – something far more important: what I call the "ultimate relationship".

What I'm talking about is your relationship with yourself. If you find yourself in a healthy, happy relationship with yourself, this will make a crucial difference to the rest of your relationships. You see, you can be single, in an unhappy relationship, or in a happy relationship. They're the three basic options. But the way you think about who you are and where you are will determine how well you're able to create the right kind of relationships with others. Most of the problems that happen in relationships and most of the reasons for people not being in happy them, boil down to ways of thinking about it. If you wonder why you keep having the same problems, relationship after relationship, it's possible that the problem is in your own relationship with yourself. Often this manifests itself in an inability to commit to the other person. Other times it's a confidence issue. But it begins with you.

I wanted to discuss this whole aspect of life once more with Richard and get his insight into the various challenges we face on the road to long-lasting love. There are all sorts of factors that affect a person's desire to find love in the modern world. Of course, circumstances are a big factor and globalisation means that we could find ourselves losing out on romance because of the nature of our career (since we might find ourselves needing to move to a new city in order to progress in our careers). One factor I've heard mentioned quite often by friends who are single is the fear of commitment. Now that we have so many choices and options, it seems that people are afraid of regretting their decisions. I wanted to see what suggestions Richard had for dealing with this.

> OF: How do you work with someone who has a problem with commitment, whereby a person might not feel able to commit to a relationship? How can you help these people to commit to things?
>
> RB: The first thing they need to be able to do is to make decisions, because if people are having trouble committing to relationships there is a good probability that they're not looking for the right person to start with. So it may be a good thing that they're not committing to that relationship.
>
> If you're not sure of what you want to start with, then you're not looking for it. People have to learn to make really big decisions, about what they like and enjoy and what type of person they want to hang around with, so that they don't meet somebody and try to turn them into somebody else.
>
> You can't have an idea and then find somebody to match your idea. You have to find out what's there, what you like and what you don't like. And when people are young they should go out and meet a really broad range of people, so that they have a lot of choice. They can find out which things they like and, the more you like it, the more you appreciate it.

Relationships should start out a little shaky and get stronger and better as they progress, not the inverse. A lot of people fall in love with an idea and not a person, in which case things get worse and they flatten out over time. If you're not thrilled to see the person you live with, that's going on inside your head too. You should feel really lucky, because there are so many lonely, miserable people on this planet.

Since the emergence of social media and our continuously expanding social circles, there seems to be more choice in potential partners than ever before. I was under the impression that the key was to limit your choices, not to have more choices. Indeed, it seems that we can suffer from what has been called "decision fatigue". But what Richard was saying made me revisit my assumption. What he was talking about is being open to the many different people in the world, instead of setting up all these rules for what the other person must be. The reality is that our idea of the perfect person is usually far removed from anyone that's actually real.

Another factor was the confidence required to approach someone you like. I asked him about this.

OF: Speaking of those lonely people, what things should they remember when they're flirting with somebody?

RB: To start with, if you're going to bother putting on fancy clothes and make-up, you should also dress up the inside of your mind. The people who attract good people are the ones who are really nice. Cheerful people attract others who are upbeat. If you go out nervous and terrified, guess what? If you attract people at all they will be just like you!

They say opposites attract, but that's not really true. People who have a lot of self-doubt will tend to find others who doubt themselves. One may be angry, the other passive, but they're both self-doubters.

Build a nice, solid foundation inside yourself. Make really solid decisions, where you know the difference between what you do and you don't believe, what you think is right and what you think is wrong, what you enjoy and what you dislike. If you make really good decisions, then, when you go out, attracting what you like is pretty easy, because you have a good idea of what you like about yourself. So then, rather than going out and trying to find someone to make you feel better about yourself than you do, you go out and demonstrate who you are and whoever's attracted to that will be drawn towards you.

One of the things I noticed, having navigated the single world for many years, is that the decisions you make are every bit as important as how good you look. Most people spend so much time trying to look good or say the perfect thing that they fail to make smart decisions or to spend time around the right kind of people. As Richard had said to me before, if you go out and get drunk, meet lots of other drunk people and find someone to be with, don't necessarily expect that person to be your ideal mate!

Part of the reason people get drunk so often is that they care so much about what people think of them. On my charisma courses I spend a lot of time helping people to be able to get over this so that they no longer need drink for this reason. This is something close to my heart, because one of the challenges I faced in the past was the experience of caring too much about what other people think. By doing so, I acted less like myself. This was an important topic.

Loving Relationships

The notion of begrudgury is one I have experienced from time to time in doing what I do. Social media tools like Facebook make it easier to see it happening, easier for people to snipe. And the truth is that the more you succeed the more you will get the attention of critics. I've had a number of stalkers and had my life threatened a few times during the course of my work. I've read about myself as being 'extremely dangerous because of my NLP skills' and had people say all sorts of things about me. I'm quite proud of the dangerous comment actually. It's kinda cool!

The truth is that the confirmation bias is largely at fault here. Once someone gets an idea into their head, they will continuously look for evidence that proves that conclusion as being true. What that means is that, often, there's nothing you can do about a person's perception of you. I have to accept that, even when I like someone and they already have an impression of me in their mind, the likelihood is that they will continue to believe what they believe. All I can do is accept it and change how I feel. I decided to ask Richard about this.

> OF: A lot of people worry that this person doesn't like me, or that person hates me, or I've got to behave like this in case this person doesn't like me…
>
> RB: Yes, that's right, because a lot of people decide how they're going to feel based on what other people think. First, they have to figure out how they think and they can't see the other person's thoughts. So half the time they're not even right: they're hallucinating that this person doesn't like them!
>
> The other person could be thinking, I need to clean my fridge and they have a funny look on their face and you look at them and go, God, he must really hate me! The trouble with using external references for things is that it's extremely unreliable and if the quality of your internal state is based on the quality of other people's external state, then that's okay; if it's your children or your wife, because you know them quite well and can read them more or less accurately – or, better yet, you can always ask!
>
> Sometimes you'll be right; other times you'll be wrong. But if you decide that you have to feel bad because somebody else doesn't approve of you, that means that you can only do things that they're going to approve of and if it's a whole lot of people they may not even agree! In which case you're in deep trouble!
>
> You need to make the reference for whether you feel good or bad based on your own internal self. If you have an idea about what the right thing to do is and you do the right thing for the right reason and feel good, that's based on an internal reference.
>
> If somebody says to you, "I'm not going to like you unless you rob a liquor store", then, with that kind of mindset, people end up robbing liquor stores! A lot of people don't take drugs just because they want to get high: they do so because they'll look bad in other people's eyes if they don't. If you have an internal reference – a compass – you just don't care. You want people to like you for who you are, not for who you can pretend to be.
>
> Understanding that and learning that is one of the hardest things for human beings, because we grow up having to seek approval to get by with our parents, our teachers. We have to please all these people along the way to get anywhere and it never stops. You have to please your employer, you have to please your audience if you lecture.

But... there are two ways of pleasing them. One: you please them by doing what they think you should do. Two: you please them by being the person who surprises everyone by sticking to your own guns. And when your guns are aimed in the wrong direction, then you holster them – and that's important, because sometimes we're just wrong. Sometimes I hurt people's feelings when I don't mean to and they tell me and then all I have to do is say, "I'm sorry" and not do it again.

When people feel guilty, they don't necessarily change their behaviour. When you notice you're doing the wrong thing, you should always feel relieved, because you don't have to make that mistake again. Relief is a much better feeling to have, as it helps you to change behaviour more easily. Unfortunately, instead people feel guilt.

You know, if I try to hypnotise somebody and my technique doesn't work I don't take it as a comment on them or a comment on me: I take it as a comment on the technique for them. So I'll try something else until I find something that works. When clients come in to me and they say, "I want everyone to like me", I go, "What an egomaniac you are! That's fucking crazy! The whole planet has to approve of you at every moment? That's a big responsibility!" And I go, "I don't approve of your wanting to be approved of. Pop it! Right on itself!"

This was another example of what Richard had discussed earlier: the use of double binds with a person's belief. The intelligence of his approach was in the idea of getting the person to think in a radically different way, not necessarily about "approval" but about the person's "desire for approval". Whenever I felt inadequate as a younger guy it was because I was trying to be like everyone else. The big realisation for me was that I didn't need to be anyone else. Even the strange, weird person I was – that was okay. It was a huge insight.

Being yourself is a cliché, but it's actually really good advice. The difficulty most people have is that they're not sure what they're supposed to do. As Richard explained, being yourself fully and completely starts by feeling really good. The better you feel, the more likely you are to be yourself. What stops people being themselves is the fear of being judged, rejected, or embarrassed. When you're feeling really good it means that you aren't feeling that fear and therefore you're far more likely to be you.

Of course, then it's also about learning to make good decisions about who you decide to spend time with. In picking friends, I make incredibly good decisions. The reason is that I typically choose friends I connect with and have fun with – friends who challenge me, who are very "real" with me and who are trustworthy and loyal. What I realised I needed to do was to start considering qualities such as these when choosing potential partners to ask out.

Once you improve the way you think about yourself, the next step is to up your game when it comes to your actual relationship with someone else. I asked for Richard's advice on this.

OF: So, how do we become better partners for the people that we're with?
RB: Well, that would depend upon the situation... That's a big question! You need to figure out what makes the other person happy and don't assume too much. And if they do something that you don't like, decide if you're going to change the way you feel about it rather than attempt to change what the other person does. If they're going to keep doing it, you might as well enjoy it!

The other thing is: speak up! Most people don't say what they really want enough, especially sexually and even with food! They pretend they like things they don't like, or they want things and they don't ask and I think this drives people apart.

If you're going to build a life together, you should build the same kinds of dreams. Find out if you're both headed in the same direction, that you want to live in the same place, that you want to have the same kinds of things. Then you can actually make compromises, but if you're always compromising without building something together . . . ! Two people together should be able to build something better than two people apart could.

I was listening intently to what Richard was saying. I knew that everything he said was what I needed to do the next time I met someone. It was really powerful advice. I wanted to continue in this theme and ask him about other important relationships that we have in life.

22. CHILDREN OF THE REVOLUTION

ON THE RTÉ TV programme *Not Enough Hours* I found myself working with a lot of families struggling with managing time and the many demands placed on them by modern life. Having children is something that changes life dramatically for couples. It's never the same again, because all of a sudden you have this beautiful little baby that needs constant attention and that you're completely responsible for.

Spending time with these families and, indeed, with my many friends who have children, gave me some insight into what it would be like to have to look after a child and an idea of what kind of effort it would involve. I would spend my time with such families playing games with the kids while the crew set up everything and the adults talked about the show.

I've always found that I get on better with children than with adults.

Children have fewer limitations in their imagination. They're more fun, more expressive, more full of life. My own two god-daughters – the two most incredibly beautiful little girls in the world, by the way – are so much fun to be around that you could hang out with them for ever.

As a therapist I've been asked to work with children quite a lot and I tend to do pretty well, because I talk to them at the same level. I understand how to get through to them. Many people don't realise that children are smarter than we give them credit for. There are four key principles I keep in mind when working with children.

1. **Consistency is key.** Whatever you say you're going to do, make sure you do it.

2. **Everything is a negotiation.** Figure out how to have them do what you want them to do by connecting it with something they want.

3. **Treat them as you want them to be.** Act as if they're going to change the behaviour you want them to change and presuppose it in how you talk to them.

4. **They learn from you,** not just from how you treat them but from how you treat yourself in front of them.

Remembering these four principles helps me to be at my most effective when working with children.

One thing I've been asked about many times over the last few years is advice for parents about using NLP with their children. I suggested my principles and stressed the importance of encouraging empowering beliefs and teaching them how to build strong positive feelings in themselves, as well as how to understand others more easily. There were so many different applications for NLP in being a more effective parent. Kate Benson, the International Director of Education for the Society of NLP and a good friend of ours, was making massive steps forward in improving how children were educated using NLP. Also, on a personal level, I had just become a godparent, so I was particularly interested in this area. I wanted to get Richard's wisdom on this.

OF: In terms of working with parents – teaching parents how to be better for their children, using NLP – what suggestions or advice do you have for them?

RB: Well, that's a complex question, because being a parent is a job that entails all kinds of things: you have to teach everything, from morals to having an appreciation for work. And then you have to teach them all the stuff that the schools don't teach them. Schools don't teach you how to spell or do art and do music. They tell you what you're supposed to do but don't share strategies with you on exactly how to do these subjects.

I think, as a parent, your job is to provide a broad range of activities for kids. When I grew up there weren't so many toys, but now there's all kinds of stuff! Make sure that your kid is as up-to-date as possible. I remember somebody getting mad because I got my kids computers – and this was twenty-five years ago. The first personal computers that came out, I shoved them right in front of my kids' faces – same with calculators! And people said, "Oh, you shouldn't do that, they should learn it the way we learnt it." But actually kids don't live in the world that we did; they grow up in a world very different from the one I grew up in. There weren't computers in everybody's houses, MP3 players and two-dollar telephones! They're going to grow up in a universe that's totally different from ours and you need to give them an appreciation for learning at a faster rate than we ever did.

I think the best thing you can do as a parent is to prepare your kids for what you yourself won't be able to cope with. Your kids have to be better prepared than you! All of us want our kids to be more successful than we are, but "success" is a funny word. Does it mean they're going to make more money than you, or does it mean they're going to be able to function better than you?

People of my generation grew up with a technology largely revolving around knobs and buttons and those days are gone. Kids growing up today need to operate in the particular world they live in. They're going to have to deal with things – gasoline is going to be really expensive. Learning to function in a world where fuel consumption has to reduce, we have to build better cars. They have different problems to the ones we had. There are more humans on this planet than there ever were, so there is more of a need for us to get along.

Obviously, the schools aren't keeping up, so we parents really have to prepare our kids to use their brains better. Part of the reason I developed the technology I did was to make up for what schools didn't do, so that we can teach kids to read and spell and do math. I'm hoping to be able to get some of this stuff productised as I go along. But even if I don't do it, I'm sure my students will. We're trying to find ways to do this. Kate Benson has done stuff for the educational system.

As a parent, you need to find out as much as you can and give as much as you can to your kids to make them better equipped than you are and I think that's the best you can do! Now, if you're living on a farm in India, then you teach them what you know and whatever new stuff is coming along. If you're living in Silicon Valley, in San Jose, then kids need to understand integrated circuit chips to get by! You don't want to teach your kids how to pick grapes in a place where there's no agriculture!

OF: Are there things that parents can encourage babies to do to maximise their learning?

RB: Well, it was discovered that babies who were carried around all the time had trouble learning to read. Apparently, crawling – and cross-crawling in particular – engages the two hemispheres of your brain and is essential for teaching the two eyes how to focus correctly so you can read. Cross-crawling is using a number of limbs at the same time while crossing the mid-point of your body. Using the right side of your body and the left side of your body in co-ordination literally helps how your brain develops. There's a thing called the "brain gym" and other techniques that can be used to give children the experience of using both sides of their brain.

In certain parts of Africa, a study showed that babies who weren't allowed to crawl around much, because of the danger of snakes in the environment they lived in, later struggled in school when learning how to read. So, first, they said that there was something wrong with the kids, but there wasn't. It was just something wrong with the way they were developing physiologically. It was something that, if they just did it, even as an adult, they would be able to pick up the patterns.

The brain just needs certain physical activity to enable the optimum performance of some mental tasks. Our body and brain aren't separate: they're all part of the same structure.

OF: To help children to grow up with a good sense of self – so that they like themselves, so that they're happy with themselves – as well as giving them specific and positive suggestions regularly such as "You're a great boy/girl because you did that behaviour", is it also a good idea for the parent to talk nicely to themselves out loud in front of the child? So when they (the parent) make a mistake, they say out loud in a nice tone of voice, "How can I do that differently next time?" so the child hears it.

RB: I think so! The warmer the tonality you use when you teach your kids things the better. When my kids did something bad I always made a distinction between what they did and who they were: "This is a bad behaviour and you're a good kid, so you shouldn't be doing it!" If you just come in and say, "You're a dumb shit and you fucked up and I hate you", pretty soon your kid is going to be thinking, I'm a dumb shit and a fuck-up and I hate myself! We're sponges: we pick up everything that's around. So you need to talk to kids in a positive voice.

A lot of people talk down to kids all the time and those children end up talking down to themselves when they go to school. They look at something and think to themselves, I could probably never do that.

I made it a policy to talk to kids the way I talk to everyone else. I think that's why I get along with patients, because I don't treat them any differently to the way I treat kids. To me, it's all about lessons and I learn as much from the people I treat as I hope they learn from me.

As I listened to Richard I couldn't but help remember how, in Harper Lee's classic *To Kill a Mockingbird*, the father character, Atticus Finch, explains that children can spot evasion quicker than most adults, so it's important to give children answers to the questions they ask.

Loving Relationships

This wisdom on handling children effectively is certainly something that can also come in extremely handy.

After listening to Richard, I had so much more that I could say the next time I was asked by parents for some NLP advice on the most effective way of helping children. I had one more question in this area. I wanted to know about talent.

> OF: I've heard you before talk about building talent. What do you mean by this?
> RB: Back in the day, when people said that somebody was talented it always sounded to me as though they were saying nobody else can do this. Yet you'd have people who were idiots doing stuff. There'd be this musician who'd be great on the guitar but couldn't function in any other area of his life! So he really wasn't brilliant; he was just talented at playing the guitar.
>
> It turns out that if somebody is a talented speller they mentally do things that are different to somebody who isn't talented at spelling. I believe the same thing is true about art, poetry, mathematics, science . . . The spirit of talent also has to have the software of talent. However, if you can add the software so that people are thinking about it the same way, that's still not enough. It needs attitude too. The fact that you so enjoy something that, when you do it, you do it completely and utterly, that's a big part of what talent is about, that sense of abandonment.
>
> I worked with a scientist when I had an optics lab and, for the guys who were there, their whole life revolved around optics. Nobody else on the planet could even understand them talk. I looked at them with awe and wonder and I always stopped to try to find out how they were thinking about these things, so that if I were going to understand them I would think about it in the same way as they did. And when I did that it always became comprehensible and it allowed me to become more talented at that.
>
> That flexibility of consciousness has always been the type of mindset that has allowed me to learn about all kinds of things. I couldn't spell when I was growing up – I can just barely spell now! – but now I know how it's done. It's still a lot of work to make pictures of words and memorise them – especially when my computer will do all the work for me at the touch of a button! But still, if we're going to teach children to spell we have to teach them how to spell. This way, we give them the chance to be talented. And the way in which one musician writes music is different from another. If we can take five, six, seven, a hundred different talented people and give them a hundred different ways of being talented and then teach people an instrument, we're going to end up with geniuses that are much more grandiose in a generation of people that can expand in an even better way.
>
> And we need to do this, especially in science! Because science has got to solve these immense problems of the planet. We're running out of energy, minerals, food and space! As soon as you start conserving things it means eventually you're going to run out. And, yes, we want renewable resources, but the best renewable resource of all will be to come up with better ways of doing things.
>
> I mean, if nuclear energy creates nuclear waste, we should be able to make it so that it's safe and create energy while we're doing it! We should be able

to come up with a better way of making electricity than steam engines, which is essentially what a nuclear power plant is – a steam engine! We should be able to create energy from the Earth, because it's spinning around. We should be able to do all kinds of wonderful things and as soon as we embrace that, we're going to start looking for that. In order to do this we need a generation of people who aren't pessimists.

The prophets of doom are everywhere, telling us everything's going to end and it's going to get worse. But guess what? They've been here since the beginning of time and they've been wrong every single time. They're going to be wrong this time. The human spirit will rise up above all difficulty and find some way to get through to the other side. Hopefully, not too many of us will be destroyed in the process!

That was it for the time being. Richard and I hung out for the rest of the day and in the back of my mind I began to dwell on what he had taught me in our conversation. I looked forward with hope to meeting someone special and possibly having children with her one day. I wondered whether or not it would happen. I resolved that if it did I would follow Richard's advice as best I could.

The next day I would continue on my journey. I knew that I would have another opportunity to ask my final questions. In many ways, they were the most important questions. I wanted to know more about some of Richard's spiritual experiences. I wanted to know about his greatest influences. It was going to be an absorbing conversation.

23. MYSTERIES OF THE HEART

THE MODERN WORLD has brought us some incredible inventions. It has transformed our idea of what's possible in technology. We now have more options available to us than ever before. If I want to watch a movie I no longer have to go to the video shop: I just have to go to iTunes and download it. If I want to listen to any song, I can do so within a matter of seconds. If I want to know about anything, I can find out, immediately.

These days our relationships have been transformed through the use of technology. We find ourselves often sitting at a table with our loved ones, all of whom have their faces lost in their phones. Louis C.K., the American comedian, suggests that the use of technology can also lead to people being meaner. Bullying through the internet is much easier because we don't have to witness the hurt of the other person, he argues. There is much truth in this. Our reliance on our contraptions is impacting the true human connections we once enjoyed. It's essential to explore how we can find our way back to appreciating such amazing parts of life and break from the addiction to "likes" and "follows".

Louis also suggests that we search for these "likes" and instant text responses from others as a way of avoiding the feeling of loneliness that has invaded the modern mind since our disconnect from the real world towards the virtual. Each positive response from others gives us a 'hit' of dopamine and serves to help us escape for just a little bit longer from the negative feelings we experience. I expect this to change however.

I believe that, as this technological age continues, we will also find ourselves entering what I call the "performance age". Our own ability to be at our best – to use our brain more effectively, to impact the world more powerfully – is critical to what's next for us. This age will teach us so much more about the most important machine ever developed – the brain – and how it's best operated. However, this age is far more complicated than the technological age. With technology, we have some semblance of control and we can predict the effect of our actions. We can't be nearly as sure when we're talking about human beings.

You see, we strive to be happy and successful. We strive to have a good lifestyle. We strive to enjoy an incredible relationship. And because, in some other areas of life, we can have so much of what we want so easily, we can get lazy. I remember Richard telling me about a client he had who was obsessed with a woman he named "Patty Perfect". The client was extremely rich and had everything he could possibly want, but he could never find a woman who lived up to this imaginary one. He was always going to be disappointed until Richard helped him see things differently and realise that he had to see the beauty in imperfection.

In today's pop culture we have a multi-billion dollar porn industry that mainly targets men. How can real women compete with an image of someone who's gorgeous and fit and who craves sex and is never moody? At the same time, there is a proliferation of books on the "ideal man". The *Fifty Shades of Grey* books and the *Twilight* series are constructing these "perfect men" who many women are supposed to desire. How can real men compete with an image of someone who's ridiculously rich and amazingly handsome . . . and whose "issues" *can* be fixed by the right woman?

Then there are these values themselves. Looks. Money. Power. Status. The beauty industry is another multi-billion industry. People spend a massive amount of hard-earned cash on clothes and personal grooming. We want to be admired. We want to be attractive. We want to be appealing.

The truth is that, these days, marketing successfully appeals to our incredible imagination. It connects products we're being sold with our ideal image of ourselves. We can have it all – if we just buy this product or that product. In the self-help industry this is as true as anywhere else. We promise happiness, success, love, health and charisma through workshops and books.

Then there is the "grass is always greener" mentality, whereby we tell ourselves that the life we haven't chosen is the better one. When you're in a relationship it can be easy to look at the single life and lament a better lifestyle; when you're single it can be easy to look at those with relationships as having it all. In reality, in whatever situation you find yourself in, it's possible for you to feel happy with it. This is an example of you "marketing" the other life to yourself. The thing is that it's always a case of what you do inside your head that gets you to feel a certain way about your circumstances and those that "might have been".

So, this leads us towards important advice that we must heed as we go into the future. It comes down to learning to accept what is happening in your life and to understanding that the choices you make will always involve having some things and sacrificing others. When it comes to love and affairs of the heart, it really is far simpler than it's made out to be.

If you're single you need to meet lots of people and be really happy with yourself when you do. You need to find someone with shared values and with whom you have a great connection. Once you're in a relationship, you need to treat each other well and be aware of the other person's goals, values and needs.

But the real secret to having a happy relationship is the relationship you have with yourself. If you're secure in yourself and who you are, you'll be in a position to have a relationship where you're both better together than apart. Most of the problems I had in past relationships came down to how I was thinking and feeling in response to the relationship and to how my partner was thinking and feeling as well.

There will always be more beautiful people in the world. There will always be people who seem happier, richer, smarter and more fulfilled. But when you can accept the fact that you're on your own journey and you're living your own life, you will find yourself having a real chance at happiness.

We tend to take so much for granted: the beauty of being free and single, the beauty of being in a committed relationship, the beauty of having children. When you remind yourself of how great you have it, you'll find yourself learning to accept the fact that sacrifices will come with the territory and that's okay. The problem most people have is that they don't think things through very well. They allow their urges or feelings to dominate the way they act. Instead, it's about being smarter by taking the view that there is a grander way to look at everything.

For example, if you think of being with someone, instead of just imagining that relationship, imagine your entire future and how it will be affected by being in a relationship with them. Imagine the good points and bad points, the great times and tough times. When you think through this filter you can get a far more realistic way of seeing the future. What this will also mean is that you will make decisions that are much better informed. Allowing your hormones, your sex drive or your "brain on infatuation" (the altered chemistry of your brain when you're in love) to make decisions isn't the smartest way of choosing what you want in your future.

This "higher level" form of thinking, I believe, is something that can have huge implications. It involves asking yourself such questions as: If I decide this, what will this really mean my life will be like? What kind of relationship would this be in reality and how will the rest of my life be affected? These questions serve to remind you of what you need to keep clear in your head. Your future depends on your ability to be clear. Clarity comes from perspective. Perspective comes from questions like these.

This is true of many other areas of life. When I was depressed all those years ago, one of the things that helped me a lot was the ability I had to go to a higher level and recognise that my emotions often create a deceptive form of reasoning. Since our minds apply cognitive distortions based on our feelings and logical fallacies, we can't always trust our judgement on the state of our lives or even what we want. To get to the real desires, we need time and perspective. So, when you feel depressed and you believe your life is screwed up, you need to step back and be aware that this is a feeling that's making everything seem that way. But it's not necessarily true: it's just a feeling. And when you're stressed and feeling like everything is going to be screwed up, it's just a feeling. This is similar to what people do when they practise "mindfulness", which is becoming more and more popular these days.

NLP helps you change your feelings so you can become smarter. But simply being aware that your mind can lie to you means that you can see through the deception. It means you can think at a higher level and ask more questions that get you thinking more strategically about the decisions you make. The ideal person doesn't exist, nor does the ideal job or ideal life. As ever, the trick is in becoming happy with what you have and where you're going. It's in being cynical enough to remember that the ideal and the real will always be different as long as we have our incredible imaginations.

All the dreams in the world can't replace the feeling of being free and single, nor can they replace the feeling of being wrapped up on the couch with your true love. So, in this reality, choose what's real. And embrace how you can make what's real even more wonderful. That's where the new focus needs to be. Instead of asking would things be better if I was living someone else's life, start asking, how can I make this life even more amazing? That way, you can enjoy spending time with whoever it is you connect with and can count yourself lucky for all you have. Besides, a porn star, vampire or sadomasochistic millionaire aren't all they're cracked up to be. I guess!

24. RANDOM RAMBLINGS: TEA WITH MY GRANNY

MY GRANNY LIVED A FEW MILES AWAY from me in Dublin ever since I was born. When I was a baby she used to help take care of me and would look after me whenever we visited her house. Every time I visited her she would sit me down at the table and insist on making me a cup of tea and rustling me up some sandwiches or cakes. If it was dinner or teatime she would insist on a meal. It didn't matter if I'd already eaten; she would still insist.

I would go over to my granny and granddad's every week and watch videos there, since we didn't have a video-player in our house. It was something I always looked forward to. When I was about twelve my granddad died. He was the first relative I was close to who passed on. It was hard. I will never forget the rainy morning when he was buried.

My granny was a fighter. She kept strong and, although she missed him terribly, kept everything running as normal. She was still the main organiser of Christmas dinner – something I looked forward to every year. It was a routine I loved. As the youngest in the family, I had the duty of harassing everyone to come into the front room, where we were to distribute the presents.

A few years later my Uncle Tony died. Granny was never the same afterwards. They say the death of your son or daughter is the worst experience there is. I can believe that.

Every Thursday I used to bring my granny out for lunch to a pub near her home called The Dropping Well. It was our routine and sometimes I'd ask her questions about her past life. Her memory wasn't always great, but sometimes she'd answer my questions with such clarity that I knew she'd had a moment of lucidity. At first her memory loss was attributed to old age. Then it got worse.

Eight years ago my granny was diagnosed with vascular dementia. She was suffering from a condition not dissimilar to Alzheimer's. At first I didn't really understand what it meant. I never really paid much attention to it. I had heard jokes about it but never really thought about it. Coming face to face with someone you love suffering from it brings home certain truths.

It's funny: even when she could barely remember who I was, she would still feel an overwhelming compulsion to make me a cup of tea. She would still insist. My granny.

Things would go from bad to worse. She became estranged from her own house and kept wanting to go home even when she was already at home. I once had to pick her up at home and take her for a drive around the area and then back home. I just walked her back into the house and she gave me a hug goodbye, delighted to be home again. I remember sitting in the car afterwards in bits. My granny.

As time went on, with Granny being cared for in a nursing home, she was safer and more comfortable but less and less aware of what was happening. There are few things more heartbreaking than looking into the eyes of someone you have loved all your life and watching them stare at you vacantly. My granny.

Loving Relationships

I soon realised that home is where the heart is . . . and where the memories are. Granny taught me the most important lesson I have ever learnt. In one of her moments of clarity, a couple of years before the onset of the disease, I asked her about her life experiences and what she had learnt. I will never forget what she said: "Memories make life wonderful."

The irony of this statement, given what soon transpired, still hurts me deep in my chest. We take for granted the moments we can remember. We go about life with an unshakeable certainty that we will always remember the events that matter the most. But that's not always the case. We must learn to cherish our moments and make every one of them count, for that's what life is about.

My granny spent the last few years residing in that nursing home. When you walk around there you're greeted with a whole host of characters who all share the same horrible affliction. It's so sad, but it teaches you something extremely valuable: remember how fortunate you are.

Look at yourself in the mirror. Do you know who you are? Do you know how you came to be who you are? Do you know your likes and dislikes, your habits and preferences? Do you know who you love in life and who loves you? Do you realise you aren't lonely, even if it feels like that sometimes? Remind yourself of that. Remember how fortunate you are.

Occasionally when I visited Granny I saw the spark of recognition in her eyes. Something deep inside her still loved me and knew that I was someone special in her life. And when that spark didn't happen my heart broke. Again.

This is what I feel. This is how I feel. It's why I embrace life-seeking adventure and challenges. I want to love every second. I want to get the most out of every moment. I want to live – really live. There is such a huge lesson in this.

When I look back at my life so far, there are so many memories that create so many kinds of feeling. One day I might not remember them. Regardless, here is the reality: even if I don't remember them, someone else may. And, no matter what, you can never take that away from me.

When a loved one passes on from this world, when a lover breaks your heart and leaves you for someone else, when a wonderful time comes to an end . . . life may never be the same again. But what happened was real and will exist for ever as part of your story. I will always remember tea with Granny. It's memories such as those that remind me to cherish the one thing that makes life worthwhile: the people we love.

On 14 June 2012, as I was on my way to the airport to go to Poland for a European Championship football game in which Ireland were playing, I got a call from my dad to say that Granny had taken a bad turn. I didn't get on the flight. I came straight back from the airport and sat by her bed with my mum, uncle and dad. We waited and watched, saying whatever we could to ensure that she was at peace, despite the fact that she may well not have heard a word. I remember her lying there, the ventilator making the only sound as her chest rose and fell. Then, with a final breath, she passed away.

Watching someone die is a surreal experience. It's something you can never forget. Something about it shifted something inside me. Watching someone slip from this world, especially someone so close . . . it changes you. You're pushed strongly towards the realisation that we all have an expiry date.

Over the next few days, memories of my time with her flooded into my mind. I learnt about everyone else's memories of her. She lived a full life.

I spoke at her funeral. It was one of the hardest speeches I've ever had to give and probably the most important. For it is in praising the legacy of a loved one that you demonstrate their immortality. For, when someone truly impacts on you, your soul is touched and it never forgets. The memory of that person will live on for ever in your mind and you will always remember their spirit. They will become immortal.

There are so many lessons to be learned from the people that we have shared this journey called life with. These stories are written so that you can gain a perspective that changes your world.

SECTION 6:
MEDICINE FOR THE SOUL

Richard's House, United States, 2011 – 2014

IT WAS SOME TIME LATER I found myself visiting Richard once again. Having arrived the night before, this was a short stop over. As I sat in his kitchen after breakfast pondering all I had learned so far, my mind began to consider yet another adventure I was embarking on and recalled some of the adventures I'd been on. One in particular stood out.

People cheering, singing, dancing like there was no tomorrow. People laughing at everything, especially at what isn't funny. People crying tears of joy and delight. Everyone hugging and jumping up and down. Love, joy, pleasure, excitement, happiness and bliss filling the room. Lovers embracing as if their lives depended on it. Kisses that last a lifetime. Musicians playing songs with everyone rocking along. Beautiful pictures everywhere. Best friends all around. No memories but wonderful ones. No fear. No sadness. No pain. No stress. Just peace. Happiness. Comfort. Calmness. Everything working out. Everything going right. Everything perfect. The kind of dream that transports you to somewhere you've never been before, yet know so well. A paradise where you feel a blend of the best feelings possible. A feeling of love for your family mixed with the feeling of falling in love, mixed with the feeling of excitement and true contentment.

A feeling of being at home with who you are, with how you are, with what you are. A feeling that everything is right and that you're perfectly safe in every way you could be. A feeling that provides you with the same kind of comfort you had years and years ago when you were very small and were cradled by your mother. When you joined your parents in bed at the age of two or three. Safe, secure, loved. The feeling when you were with someone you were crazy about and you had your head on their chest or theirs on yours. You felt them breathing and felt like you belonged there, simply listening to their heartbeat, wishing it would last for eternity. No worries about the future. No disappointments. No regrets. Nothing but being in the moment and simply knowing, somehow, that everything will work out okay. It's this kind of feeling we all crave. And yet, somehow, paradoxically, life interferes.

I experienced this feeling in its purest form. It happened one day in February 2006. I had experienced a shamanic ritual in the hills of Quito, near the Amazon rainforest. It was one of the most surreal and powerful experiences of my life.

Five years later, as Richard and I sat in his office for the final time on my visit, I began the process of finding out more about his own experiences in South America.

25. THE WISDOM OF A SHAMAN

IT WAS A SATURDAY MORNING at the end of February in Ecuador. I had just finished teaching a three-day course on "The Art of Charisma" to about fifty participants in the centre of Quito. Today was an exciting day. I was off to meet a shaman in the hills of the city.

I was picked up from my hotel at 7 a.m. We set off, collecting my interpreter on the way. I was tired but excited. I had a feeling that things were going to be very interesting. Little did I know that I was about to experience something that would change how I viewed the world for ever.

The road got progressively bumpier and the surroundings progressively greener. There were fewer and fewer cars on the road. We travelled for a couple of hours. Then, finally, in the middle of nowhere, we arrived.

I met the small group. Through my interpreter, they explained the process. There would be many rituals. They would involve mushrooms and the ayahuasca plant. I was intrigued. I felt adventurous. I was up for it. Two shamans would be leading the ceremony. One of them was a tall, thin, pony-tailed man in his mid to late fifties who resembled a slightly darker and thinner version of Steven Seagal. The other was shorter and in his sixties, with a full head of curly grey hair.

We began by sitting down inside a hut, chanting for a while. Then we were brought mushrooms and honey. The horrendous taste of the mushrooms, which seemed to be freshly picked, explained the honey. We consumed a number of these and waited as the shamans continued to chant.

After we had spent some time sitting around the fire in a circle, next to the wood, with two drummers tapping a hypnotic rhythm, my senses started to give way. I began to experience a heightened state of awareness and felt completely transfixed by the beat. This sensation was a radical departure from normal consciousness, but it was nothing close to what was to come.

We were then given a drink, a psychoactive decoction fermented from the ayahuasca vine and some almost equally horrendous-tasting alcohol to wash it down with. I say almost, because ayahuasca was the most disgusting drink I've ever had in my life!

It was then, as I've heard Richard beautifully describe it once before when talking about a trance state, that "the world came apart at the molecule". To this day, I fail to find the words to describe the experience. I found myself with an incredible urge to smile and to smile blissfully. I began to smile so hard I couldn't help laughing. At nothing. Absolutely nothing. Just laughing, over and over again. Everything was funny. Everything was hilarious. Even the banal was hysterical.

For a short time everyone around me turned into dragons and monsters and yet I didn't care. Then they turned into pizzas that wanted to eat me and I simply laughed. My brain was releasing feel-good chemicals by the gallon, it seemed and I was giggling away, unable to stop.

This was soon converted into a warm feeling and glow – a feeling of complete home. If you can imagine the most intense love, a feeling of warmth and complete security and pure bliss all mixed together – that's similar to what I experienced. It was spellbinding.

Medicine for the Soul

Next, it felt as if my brain were transported through time. I saw every moment of my life flash before my eyes. I got to look back at every experience I could think of and experience it again, but with this amazing feeling accompanying it.

One by one, my negative memories and experiences transformed in front of my very eyes. It was the ultimate "change personal history"! I felt forgiveness towards people who had wronged me, especially myself. My memories – my past – were being cleaned and freed from negativity. I was in heaven.

This heaven included flashbacks, but instead of remembering how all the good memories ended, I experienced them as a series of present moments. I also felt like I talked to God and as I looked around I saw the energy of the world. I finally understood what all the gurus and spiritual teachers had been talking about when they described the beauty of the now.

Ayahuasca means "spirit of the vine". It's used to help people experience enlightenment, understand the true nature of the universe and connect with spiritual beings. On that day in February I experienced all of that and more. Unfortunately, the process also included a "purging" of toxins. Purging, as far as I can make out, is another way of saying "projectile vomiting" . . . This was the least pleasant part of the experience. And after the "purging" there was a darkness to the experience – a feeling of being trapped inside my own mind. But thanks to my previous experience with hypnosis and altered states I made it through that part okay.

Of course, some people will consider my experience to be the product of hallucination as a result of experimenting with chemicals. There will be those with a black-and-white view of the subject. However, it really depends on your viewpoint. From the sceptic's point of view, such plants induce hallucinations and you see and hear things that aren't there, because reality is distorted.

But the shamans I was with believe the opposite. They believe that the world we live in is the distorted world and that it's only when you use the plants God gave you that you can actually see and hear the real world – the spirit world. It's a matter of perspective. In other religions and spiritual beliefs, such as the Rastafari movement, substances like cannabis are part of the spiritual practice and aid the healing of the spirit. This experience for me was certainly highly spiritual.

Regardless of what the reality is or was, one thing was for sure: I would never look at my life in the same way again. I wanted to know more about how Richard had been affected by his experiences meeting shamans.

> OF: Richard, you've travelled around the world; you've met many different people. I've heard you discuss some of the experiences you had when you went to visit the shamans in North and South America. What do you think was the biggest lesson you learnt in your time in that part of the world?
>
> RB: Well, that would depend upon whom I was with. You know, I went to very different parts of North and South America. I still think one of the most interesting people I met was up behind the river in San Blas, in Mexico. He was a real quirky kind of a guy. He used personal magick with the local population, mostly as what I would call "problem-solving".
>
> People would come to him either with family issues or health problems or financial problems and he would create for them basically what we would call a totem or a magickal object – sometimes it would be something as simple as a rock – and he would cast spells over it. I found that most of these objects were designed to get people to have confidence in what they were doing, whether

they were trying to recover from an illness or, you know, catch more fish. If they had some magickal object on which they focused their attention and built a powerful belief, then that's it: they were going to catch more fish. Then they had a tendency, I believe personally, to try harder.

And I think that's what the magick was. Scientists will argue whether the magick was in the rock or whether the magick was in the belief. I know, with things like the placebo effect, that doctors are always worried about what's real. I was told originally that placebos work because people are deceived – that they believe that there's a drug there when there isn't a drug. I personally don't think that matters. I personally have found that if people believe that it's a placebo and you prove to them how well placebos work, then they work even better. This seems crazy, but it's the act of believing that creates magick and whether that's done with a pill or an object doesn't seem to matter so much to me.

Whereas most shamans have a particular thing – they would always build people the same object – this guy would pick pretty much anything – a piece of bone, of crystal, or whatever. He would perform a whole ritual around it with whoever the person was, or sometimes he would get the whole family, sometimes the whole tribe and they would perform a whole ritual of chanting, where everybody would focus their attention. He would call the spirits down and get the spirits to charge up the crystal, or the rock, or the bone, or whatever it was.

But the amount of time that he spent creating an altered state for people – not just the person, but the people around him – to believe that it would work meant that everybody would envy the guy who had the object as he walked by with it around his neck on a string. You could tell that, when he walked through, his peers would all look at him with envy, because he had this magickal power now and that allowed him to be better at what he had to do. And this particular guy went out and caught snakes, which I think personally you have to have a tremendous amount of courage to do – or a tremendous amount of stupidity. Maybe some combination of both.

I didn't speak the language of these people, so everything I had to observe was outside of the domain of words. This was watching people talk to each other, listening to their tones, watching their faces, their eyes, seeing the altered state that surrounded the whole ritual they performed. And I think that what people forget when they do things that are "communication arts" – whether it's a medical doctor talking to a patient, whether it's a psychotherapist talking to a patient, or a neuro-linguistic programmer helping a client, or whether you're doing sales trading – is that these events are rituals very much like shamans perform. Part of it is magick, part of it is skill and the whole package surrounding these things that gives people something magickal to take away is a belief.

I've read books in the domain of the occult dating back hundreds of years saying that when people took rings and totems and they performed rituals and bestowed magical powers, they basically got people to believe that if they wore this ring certain things would happen – that they would have certain abilities. Whereas in the movies they make it so that it's the ring that does it, it's really your belief in the power of the ring – the power of the object; the power of the learning.

When someone who works with magick takes some kind of magickal power and sticks it in an object, I don't believe that is a separate act from the act of people believing that it's there. When you take all the minerals that constitute a human being and all the fluids that constitute a human being and it's born, you could take all those same elements that constitute the body and it could be a pile of goop and bones on the floor. But the fact that it has ideas, that it can think, that it has a brain, that it believes things, that it has a birth and death is a magickal phenomenon. When people forget that, they forget to deal with people as magickal beings.

One of the big learnings that I got was that instead of it just being procedures, where NLP was just following steps until something happens, it becomes more important the way you do it. You get people involved and you get them to believe that what they're doing is going to work and that you're installing in them an idea and that idea is an "elemental". I don't do ring magick, I don't stick ideas in stones and I don't give people magickal crystals to wear; but I give them beliefs where you put magickal powers inside of an idea and it alters the way people live.

OF: Well, except for grapes. I've seen you charge grapes.

RB: Yes, well, it's a grape day to be alive!

During a course, Richard would often take a grape and explain that he had put a good feeling into it so that when someone ate it they would have an unexplainable sense of well-being. Sometimes after doing a demonstration on stage he would hand the person the grape and tell them that it would make them feel "grape"! Sure enough, a bright smiled beamed on the person's face as soon as they swallowed the grape.

What I found fascinating about Richard's explanation was that he was emphasising the unique power of the mind – the power of belief. Much of the work you do is with beliefs. You get your client to believe that your company sells the best products. You get your patient to believe that this is the best medicine. You get your audience to believe that this show will be fantastic. It's all about beliefs.

Now, I've found that in the spirituality industry there are many people who profess their "powers". These "Harry Potter wannabes", as I like to call them, act as if they're sending energy bolts to the people around them. You'll spot them walking around like they're enlightened and moving their hands in weird shapes, as if they're actually throwing energy around.

When Richard referred to "magick" he was not referring to magic as performed by stage magicians but rather to a spiritual process in which you use the power of your "will" (and imagination) to change the world. Richard had explained that, in reality, real magick comes from belief. That doesn't make it any less magickal. Indeed, it makes it even more magickal, because the real spiritual leaders, the real energy-healers or shamans or gurus all have one thing in common: they have inspired belief in a group of people.

It seems like all religious and spiritual practices involve a level of belief and a set of rituals that the followers engage in. Whether you call it "meditation", "journeying", or "praying"; whether it's directed at the Earth and moon, God, Jesus, or Buddha; whether it involves a number of chants repeated over and over or is designed to focus on a particular idea – it's all the same kind of thing. It involves using your mind to make a connection with something bigger and more powerful. It involves altering your reality.

26. ALTERING REALITIES

SCIENTISTS HAVE ARGUED that they've found the "God spot" in the brain. By stimulating a part of the brain, they found that it is possible to give people a "spiritual experience". This would fit quite nicely with their suggestion that the psychoactive substances do something similar and thus cause us to hallucinate. However, to me, this is missing the point.

As I listened to Richard I was asking myself how his experiences and my experiences had happened and what they meant. For years science tried to nail down "reality", until quantum mechanics came along and messed it all up. The reality is that we don't know what reality is. Indeed, mainstream movies such as *The Matrix* have explored philosophical notions that suggest that our perceptions do not reveal reality.

When I was experiencing the influence of ayahuasca it certainly felt real to me. My reality for that Saturday was altered. It was significantly different from what I normally experienced on a Saturday. I mean, Glasgow Celtic winning usually gives me some degree of delight, but never that degree.

In many ways, the act of cheering Celtic on was itself a magical experience. We walk the long pilgrimage, usually in the freezing cold, from the centre of Glasgow to the stadium, in an area called Parkhead. Then we stand together chanting our own songs, hoping and praying that we will emerge victorious. All that energy focused on Celtic. All that love focused on Celtic. And, like the shamanic experience, some form of bliss (followed by nausea if we lose!).

The power of beliefs is obviously an important component in spiritual practice. Another part of my shamanic experience that I wanted insight about was the power of altered states. I asked Richard about this.

> OF: You've had quite a lot of experience in terms of trance and altered states. What made you interested in shamans and witch doctors? And what kinds of experiences and memories did you bring back that taught you things and enabled you to enhance the quality of people's lives?
>
> RB: As soon as I started learning hypnosis I realised that the things that were going on, the things that I had seen Milton [Erickson] and Virginia [Satir] do and the things that I had seen people in therapy going through, were in fact trance states – whether they call it "meditation" or "centering".
>
> In the course of these types of psychotherapies, for the part of it where profound change occurred, people were actually in altered states. You could call them altered states, trance states, or meditative states.
>
> You can measure brain waves. My fascination right now is with designing machines that can affect brain activity – things like the "mind spa" and some of the new devices I'm working on that are literally going to build loops into the brain so that the machine actually responds strategically to changes that occur.
>
> This idea dates back to over forty years ago, when I used to go and study psychotherapists to find out how they were changing people. But I also hung

out with gurus from various religions. I met shamans in India, in the Amazon and Native American witch doctors. They don't call them witch doctors there, but that's basically what they are.

I consider being a witch doctor a good thing, by the way. That's one of the criticisms I would hear from psychiatrists – you know, putting somebody down and calling him a witch doctor because he used hypnosis. But yet, witch doctors can get some pretty profound results!

When I studied Voodoo I didn't study it because I wanted to curse people: I studied it because in such religions they induce powerful changes in people. If that's what it takes to get rid of somebody's fear or depression – if you call somebody's depression a curse – and you remove the curse and the person is happy, I'm satisfied with that! I don't need causation; I don't need to term mental things in pseudo-science.

I think psychiatry really wanted it all to boil down to mental things having nuts and bolts, so to speak. In medicine, you find a virus, you get rid of the virus. Same with bacteria, or tumours. People would always return to that medical underpinning of psychiatry, since they had all become doctors first!

In social sciences they tried to pretend to be hard sciences and they didn't even know how to do it. That was the problem: you don't do statistical studies and come out with hard science. The mathematics of science predict things exactly; they don't predict things some of the time. "Some of the time the plane will take off and some of the time it won't" would never be good enough! We want precise predictions: "Do this and this happens."

With humans and their mental phenomena, the sum is always greater than the parts. You can't spell if you don't visualise the words and copy them down. It's that simple. If you take kids who are "learning-disabled" and you teach them to make eidetic-remembered images and you go through the procedures to do that, they'll end up being able to spell words. And it won't matter whether they're big words or little words, because this idea that words have grade levels is nonsense. They're either pictures or they're not pictures!

And some languages, like German, you can almost spell phonetically, but certainly in English you don't stand a chance. It's just not a very phonetic language. We have silent letters. You know, words like "caught". It's just not phonetic!

When I went and looked at shamanic states I was also looking at other trances and finding out how they used those other trances. I saw a lot of things that I just couldn't explain, but I also saw a lot of things that I could use.

A lot of the ways I induce trances are very similar to the way in which the gurus I met in India did. They breathe at the same rate, they go into deep trances very suddenly and they touch people on the forehead and I do much the same thing with my students.

They breathe at the same rate as people and at the very moment that they start to go into an altered state they'll jump into a heightened state of bliss themselves and people will have the best feeling they've ever had – because a lot of people haven't had a lot of experience with good feelings! – whereas these people who have been meditating for years, since their childhoods, are very good at getting into pleasant states.

> If you breathe at the same rate as somebody and alter your state, typically people will go with you. I saw lots of shamans using that principle, as an opening where they created a state and got people to follow them. They did this to me in India, over and over again! I'm just not a good joiner. I'm a really good quitter, but I'm not a good joiner! But I did take away with me the ability to do that.
>
> Now I don't want followers: I'm just not that sociable. But I used it as a vehicle to get people into altered states very rapidly and I used this over years to do profound things with them.

One thing in particular struck me about what Richard had been continually saying. To him, theories and labels and "who was right" didn't matter. What mattered was what worked. From the mechanics of a clock to the practice of Voodoo, Richard was interested in how things worked, how they stopped working and, most importantly, how to get them back working again.

It was a radically different approach to the area of personal change. As a psychologist I've spent many years understanding the theories and academic underpinnings of psychological concepts. I've compiled statistical analyses and created theses laden with references. I understand the need for such reports in certain situations, of course, but it occurred to me that we don't need all that research to tell us what we can understand through our experience.

The magick that seems to happen as a result of religion or spirituality is often dismissed by scientists as being the result of coincidence or pure belief. But this presupposes that pure belief is out of the sphere of magick. What I was taking from Richard was that, instead of trying to find ways to argue that magick doesn't exist, we should look at all the magickal things that do exist and that we take for granted.

If people with terminal illnesses can experience spontaneous remission and the common denominator suggests that they believed that they would get better, that's quite a dramatic result. One thing I know from my own therapeutic practice is that the key for me was beliefs. I needed to get the person in front of me to believe that they could change and would change and that the technique or work I was doing with them would lead to this change. Then they needed to believe that the change would be permanent.

What is interesting is that, no matter how weird the therapeutic approach, they all work on someone in some way. That's how they generally become known. One of the reasons NLP is so popular is that the techniques, instead of working only for those who are really good, actually work for almost anyone who practises them. But for you to be able to help people change, they have to believe it's possible.

The magick of believing in objects is not much different from the magick of believing in yourself. When you do, amazing things are possible.

The concept of energy isn't widely considered in Western medicine, but it's an integrated part of Chinese medicine. One of the things the renowned creativity expert Edward de Bono once told me at an innovation panel we were both consultants on was that a big problem that modern society has is this need to be right. In his book *Why So Stupid?*, he argues for a different way of thinking about what we don't understand. The notion that Western medicine has to be right and Eastern medicine wrong is simply not useful and not accurate. The reality is that it's only in opening yourself up to more possibilities that you can find the real magick in life.

Medicine for the Soul

Richard chatting with Swami Sukhabodhananda in Bangalore, India

Trekking through Central America

27. HEALING THE PLANET

AS EVER, I found myself fascinated by Richard's experiences and feeling so grateful that stories such as these had inspired me to travel the world and experience all I had experienced. But I wanted a little more. I wanted to know what other kinds of experiences Richard had had with the spiritual gurus and shamans he spent time with.

OF: Is there a particular memory you have of something especially wacky or crazy that the shamans did?

RB: Well, it really comprises quite a circus of things over the years. I remember being with Yogi Bhajan in an ashram in San Francisco and I literally brought a laser and a hologram with me and I showed them to him. There were all these people there in their little turbans and their white suits, sitting around in a circle on Persian rugs. Yogi and I were in the middle, with a laser in between us. I showed him a hologram I had of three chess pieces and a magnifying glass. When you look at it, if you tilt your head a certain way, it magnifies all three pieces one at a time. It's not like looking at a picture: it's like looking at three chess pieces through a magnifying glass! I chopped it in half and had him look at it and none of the images were cut. When you cut a hologram the image stays the same, but the amount of brightness is diminished as you reduce the size.

As he looked at it, he turned around to me very nonchalantly and said to me, "So the knowledge of the magnifying glass is on every molecule", and I said, "Yes." He says, "Oh, I understand that. I've understood that for many years."

Then I asked him, "If the laser beam shines through your aura, does it change you?" In order to answer that question he of course has to be able to see my aura, so while he was doing that I breathed at the same rate as him and went into an altered state like he did and when I did it – *boom!* – I could suddenly see auras extremely brightly for the first time in my life, because of the state I was in! As bright and distinct as the colours in a painting.

That was a profound experience. I haven't found a lot of use for it, but it's certainly a memorable experience for me!

Yogi Bhajan was an exceptional guy. He did trippy things. I saw him yelling and screaming at somebody for something and then just suddenly walking over and putting his hands on their head and they went from being all freaked out to being totally calm. You could say it was an anchor, you could say it was a post-hypnotic suggestion, or you could say that perhaps he knew how to take energy and move it from himself to another person.

Those are just descriptions. When I see things, I don't worry about the description of it or how it's labelled. I concern myself with learning how to do it.

> Many of the things I saw in India I have no idea how they were done and I haven't been able to re-create them. One guy in India took this tiny little candle and got a huge flame to come out of it. Stage magicians have told me you can do that by dropping chemicals in the air and I'm sure you can. But I've studied stage magic close up and this guy had no chemicals. Maybe there was something I didn't know about; maybe there was a gas leak in the floor. I don't know. But what I saw was impressive. I don't go about trying to explain it: I go about trying to learn to do it. Some I've been able to do. Some I haven't.
>
> To me, when I spent time with the Indians the most impressive part of the ritual was that they made it rain in the middle of the desert. It took a long time – days! Lots of chanting and singing and a big fire. I do remember that they got it to rain, with lightning and everything. I asked the old Indian how he made it rain and he replied that making it rain is easy, but getting the clouds to come is hard!

My mind went back to my experience in the Amazon. What I had seen there had a significant impact on how I saw the world. But, to me, this was an even more beautiful idea. Richard talked about how such rituals changed the world.

With the environmental challenges we face, with the greenhouse effect, with stranger weather coming every year, with volcanoes exploding and grounding flights, with hurricanes and tornadoes, tsunamis and earthquakes, it seems that the world is in revolt.

Then there are human beings. We chop down forests and pollute the atmosphere. We bury rubbish and kill animals to eat. We eat food that's bad for us and fail to exercise. We attack people who don't share our beliefs and we watch as our fellow-humans rape, steal and murder. We wage full-scale wars that kill millions of people and justify it by saying that we were on the "right" side. We wonder why bad things happen and then we talk about the concept of "humanity".

The truth is that there needs to be a shift. There needs to be a change. Not just a change in policy but a change in philosophy. There needs to be a movement. Not another movement *against* something but a movement *for* something. A movement for a new way of thinking – for a new perspective on the world. Many have called for it and it hasn't happened. But we need to keep calling.

You see, I'm an optimist grounded in reality. I'm a cynic grounded in faith. I'm right in the middle. I have friends who talk to angels and friends who live by the rules of science. The way I see it is that whatever you believe will determine your reality. So I choose to be open to possibilities but convinced of much less. What I do believe in is the ability we have to do far more than what we have managed to date.

We've built rockets that have been fired into space. We've managed to connect to people on the other side of the planet for real-time conversations. We've cured diseases and made a huge difference to millions of people's lives. We fly thousands of miles in metal tubes and we've built gravity-defying buildings and amazing technological marvels. We're capable of so, so much.

If shamans can make it rain, what else is possible for us? What would truly be great is if we could learn to make the sun shine. To me, that's what my job is all about. That's what I've been learning over the years from Richard: to make the sun shine in people's lives, to reach out and connect with our fellow-humans and understand the universal truth that we're all the same and we're all unique and to know that this paradox makes everything more beautiful.

Richard has had such an influence on me. I began to wonder who the main people who really influenced him were.

28. THE GREAT INFLUENCES

THE NAMES that had cropped up time and time again, every time NLP was discussed, were Fritz Perls, Virginia Satir and Milton Erickson. I wanted to find out who the other great influences were, both at the time and since then – those who had helped shape how Richard thought. During the earliest years, Richard and John were encouraged and supported by one of the leading thinkers in social science, Gregory Bateson.

OF: What are the biggest lessons you've learnt from the memories you have of Gregory Bateson and your interactions with him?

RB: Well, I'd read Gregory before I met him and Gregory's work was very impressive, because I don't know how an anthropologist became so good. I mean, when he analysed Nazi war films and propaganda and all kinds of stuff. He grew out of that history of studying Wittgenstein and all of these great thinkers that learnt to take language and quantify and qualify it.

Gregory went a step further in terms of looking at how it affected behaviour. He worked at the Mental Research Institute. This is where Jay Haley and John Weakland were, who were trying to do something called "brief therapy". Brief therapy was ten sessions and in those days that was killing the sacred cow. Therapy was supposed to take five years and still never accomplish anything, because people weren't supposed to change.

He was the first one to examine Milton Erickson's work and to take a look at different therapies and different things and to figure out that the context in which something occurred had more to do with understanding the communication than anything else. Now, whereas some of his students said I didn't understand Gregory, Gregory thought I understood him perfectly. And he understood when I talked to him.

When he read our first book, *The Structure of Magic*, he went, "Wow, this is what we were trying to do. We were trying to look at the process instead of the content." And Gregory was the process guy about language. He understood that the "double bind" is what kept schizophrenics schizophrenic: you were sick for not admitting you were sick. So if you were in the mental hospital and said, "I don't belong here", they went, "Oh, his symptoms are getting worse." Gregory's descriptions of how double binds from families and stuff made people crazy I think are really important.

But the best thing about Gregory is the conversations. We had long conversations. We'd play chess and drink martinis. Gregory had been everywhere and done all kinds of stuff, but he understood that when you dealt with ideas you tried them on to find out whether or not they worked. We even went back and examined what he discovered in his research and asked, "If you had known the meta-model, would they have been different?" We took some of his meta-dialogues and re-examined them using the meta-model. And, you

Medicine for the Soul

know, it produced different results and different outcomes. He is everything that an intellectual should be, in my mind. And he was a real pleasure to know.

OF: Most people who have heard of NLP will have heard of Gregory Bateson, as well as Fritz Perls, Virginia Satir and Milton Erickson. Who else did you model?

RB: Well, there's Moshé Feldenkrais. I met Moshé, I think, in the late 1970s in Chicago and he came to a seminar because his students were learning this NLP stuff and he wanted to show them that it was a bunch of nonsense. And he came in and sat in the third row and I talked for maybe forty-five or fifty minutes and this fat little pudgy guy with grey hair jumped up out of the audience, walked up on the stage and started scolding everybody for not seeing how important this was. And I had no idea who he was. Or why he was standing on the stage with me. But the one thing I noticed right away was everybody was really listening to this guy. I literally asked him, "Who are you?" "I'm Moshé Feldenkrais." I knew him, because I'd talked to students of his.

One of Moshé's students had tried to get me to model Moshé's work for a long time, but I was, to tell you the truth, sick of people who did bodywork, because most of the time I'd go through these long, arduous things where I'd be no better off and they'd try to convince me that I was. I just didn't like the whole nonsense. They spent too much time in health-food stores wearing pyjamas in those days.

Nowadays, people who do those kinds of things are much more precise. You go into a health-food store and they know what they're talking about in terms of chemistry. Back in those days they just thought it was good to eat a lot of carrot juice. In fact, many of them had orange fingertips because they drank too much of it!

Finally, I saw films of Moshé working with people. I remember very vividly watching Moshé work with three different clients. One had multiple sclerosis and was so crippled she could barely move. She came in on a walker, moving at the speed of a snail and her knees had knocked together so much while walking, because they were so contorted that they were talking about cutting this person's tendons in order to straighten out her legs.

There was a doctor there talking about the surgery they were going to do. Moshé put this woman on a table with her legs bent and had her push her knees together and put his hands in between the knees and pushed out while she squeezed her knees together. Then he put his hands on the outside of her legs and had her push her knees out. And the whole time he was chit-chatting with her and humming a waltz. After doing this for a period of time, he laid her on her side and gently pulled her hip back and was just humming and singing and rolled her on her other side and pulled her head back. He spent maybe thirty minutes doing this.

All of a sudden he takes her legs and swings her round and stands her up straight as a board and starts dancing with her! And there are nine hundred people in the audience. You could see that probably about seven hundred of them had tears coming out of their eyes. But I remember being ultra-impressed by it and that's when I decided that we'd start to work together.

I remember I had just bought my house in Santa Cruz in 1976. Just after the house was finished being remodelled, Moshé came to stay with me. He stayed there for about a month and I brought clients in and did all kinds of things. I helped him publish a couple of books, including *The Elusive Obvious*. He had some trouble with his publishers. They wanted to change the books, so we took the books and I eventually published the books through Meta Publications.

Moshé taught me a lot about the human body – how it moved – but he didn't do body therapy. He talked about what he did as giving people lessons in movement. You're teaching the body to do something. He told me his great epiphany was when he worked with somebody that had been attacked in a Palestinian raid. He was a flautist in the Jerusalem Philharmonic and he'd been shot in the wrist and they'd cut the nerves in his arm.

Microsurgeons went in and did all the repair that they could do and they told him he'd never play again. The guy came to see Moshé to see if there was anything that could be done. Moshé thought to himself, how could this guy know what the notes sound like and not be able to make them? So he taught him a new way to hold the flute. And had him move the flute so that if he couldn't press his finger down he would twist the flute in a certain way and it would push against his finger. And he did this whole thing and five months later this guy was playing solos in front of the Philharmonic.

Moshé at that point decided there isn't anything that the body can't learn to do in a new way. If there is severe damage it requires new lessons; with a lot of people they simply had never learnt to do things.

I remember he asked me questions: "Do you know how to blow your nose?" And I said, "Of course I do." And he said, "Show me." And I blew my nose and he said, "That's silly: you just blew your nose and then sucked all the snot back up your nose deeper into your sinuses." He said that if you want to blow your nose, you hold the rag off your nose, with the snot on your nose; you inhale through your mouth; you blow out through your nose; and inhale through your mouth again so that it creates the suction. That's the way the body is designed.

There are lots of nice things about the way the body's designed, like the fact that your nose is over your mouth. It's such a better place to have it than it being over your butt. That way you can smell what goes in and when you smell, it adjusts all the saliva – all the things in your metabolism to digest that food – rather than if it was over your ass. Then all you'd ever be able to do is have regret! Many people don't smell their food on the way in. If you think about where the nose is placed, every spoonful of food you smell through your nose and then taste, not only are you going to know more about tasting your food, but you're going to make better decisions about what you're going to put in your mouth.

OF: What are your memories of other people who influenced you?

RB: Well, I had a philosophy professor in college whose name was William Tuttle. I found him incredibly impressive, because part of the way he taught people philosophy was that he would come in and he would become the philosopher and he would defend their point of view, no matter what it was. He would take every side and every argument that had been going on in philosophy since the beginning of time. He'd read these things and understood them well enough and he didn't argue about it as if it was ancient history. He would argue about it as if it were today. So he would become Aristotle, but he would talk about current events. People would bring in newspaper articles and file them on his desk and he would come up and announce who he was out of the things we'd read and he would discuss the issues of current times as the philosopher.

He's also the first person that introduced me to mathematical logic. I'd read about things like that and read Aristotelian logic and things like this, but he was the first person I'd ever met that applied it. He would literally take newspaper articles and write out syllogisms, predicate calculus of these things, compute the validity of the arguments and show the logical fallacies that came up in people's thinking. So he did it with political figures and it was very funny, but he was a very bright guy. He showed me how you could try on thinking and how it would work and with very divergent thinking you could think like a different person and try on something.

Later in life, when I started discovering things about strategy, it became my way of knowing whether you had all the pieces. You could try on a different motivational strategy than your own and see if it would work, what the upside and what the downside would be. That ability to try on a set of perceptions and a set of thinking skills is something definitely that I got from him.

Someone else who influenced me was the guy that I learnt martial arts from when I was a kid. His philosophy was just absolutely funny. He's the guy that punched a hole through an eight-inch plywood with his hand and we were all totally impressed and gasping and he turned around and said, "You know, I spent twenty years learning to be able to do that and never once have I been attacked by plywood." He did everything in his power to get us to start to laugh at the futility of anything. Every movement, everything you did, should be functional in some way.

He'd bring in these big, fancy martial arts things, with chains and sticks and he'd do exquisite things with them, but he didn't need to. He'd pick up a plate, throw it like a frisbee and break a brick in half with it. "One of those to the throat and the fight's over!" he'd say. His attitude was that everything around you could be used. To me, that's drifted over into everything I do. Everything people say and think, I try to use in a way to create that moment of paradox where they can escape their model of the world and build one that's more functional.

OF: Someone else that you've talked about many times is Robert Anton Wilson.
RB: Yes, absolutely. Robert Anton Wilson was my good friend. I'd read Robert for years before I met him and Robert just has a real different view of the world. He was one of the smartest and most educated people I'd ever met in my life. You could mention anything and Robert knew something about it. He was just one of the most well-read people. I used to make stuff up just to see, to try and stump him. I'd go, "Flying monk", and he'd go, "Yes, 1491", and then start naming times and dates and places. He was one of those people that paid attention to all the details of everything.

I remember him reciting a poem one day. We went out for Chinese food. When I met Robert he could walk, but later in life he lost the use of his legs. I had a station wagon. I got nine people in the station wagon, with his wheelchair strapped to the roof. When everybody got out and went inside for Chinese food, I got the wheelchair off the roof, got Robert out of the car and put him in the wheelchair. It was a lovely, balmy night in southern California. He stopped to smoke a cigarette, looked up at the stars and started reciting this poem. And it went on and on and on. It was beautiful. It was just one of those magical moments in life.

I turned to Robert and I said, "How can you remember all of those words so precisely?" and Robert looked up and said, "Because it's written in the sky." He literally held his hands about twelve inches apart and goes, "In my memory, a line of poetry is about this big. When I sit here I could look up in the sky and I see it and it scrolls up a bit like the thing in the beginning of *Star Wars*, I guess."

I remember thinking at that moment, gosh, if they'd have taught me to do that in school, I'd have had a much better memory. Nobody ever taught me to do that. They always said to learn poetry, but they never told you how to memorise all those words or how big the letters should be. The fact that it was written by some guy who died three hundred years ago didn't matter, because when he read it he had a certain feeling attached to it.

Robert was a wonderful guy. I don't think in ten books I could tell you all the things that I learnt from him. He was, hands down, the smartest man I ever met in my entire life. For people reading this who haven't read Robert Anton Wilson's books, they're all so different, from science fiction and all the way up through things that could be considered psychology and beyond. Robert is just

Richard with Robert Anton Wilson in the good old days

> a bright guy. Books like *Prometheus Rising*, you know, it's not so much what he is saying: it's what it does to your mind in the act of reading it.
>
> It's like, my daughter was trying to read *Finnegans Wake* or *Ulysses*. She said she was having trouble and I said, "Well, read it out loud with an Irish accent. It's made to be read out loud with an Irish accent. Then it will make more sense." *Ulysses* is about language. It's a fascinating thing to think that six hundred books have been written about the six books that one guy wrote. *Ulysses* and *Finnegans Wake* are works of art in language. And for those of us who are wordsmiths there are places to look. To me, the two great wordsmiths aren't who most people think they would be: I think it's definitely James Joyce and Robert Anton Wilson. When you read their books out loud the language weaves a trance unlike any other. Milton [Erickson] was pretty good with language, I have to admit. He was, in the land of therapists, the best. But Robert Anton Wilson could induce much deeper and stranger states than Milton Erickson could even conceive of.

Indeed, Robert Anton Wilson had a huge influence on me as well. I was lucky enough to meet him on a seminar he spoke at in California in 2000, with Richard in an NHR training he did with John LaValle. I had read Robert's books already and found his ideas commanding my attention and ensuring that I never thought the same way again.

Richard is perhaps the most significant influence I've had in my career and in my development since meeting him back when I was just a teenager. The lessons I've learnt from him are too vast to state in one chapter. Indeed, most of *Conversations* and the book you hold in your hands represent just some of the wisdom that has profoundly affected and transformed my life.

There are many others: my direct trainers John and Kathleen LaValle, who have taught me so much about language and business; Eric Robbie, who taught me to pay more attention; Paul McKenna, who taught me about performing effectively; Michael Breen, who taught me to be more expressive on stage; Joe Keaney, who taught me how to use hypnosis in therapy; Tony Robbins, who taught me the power of enthusiasm; Jim Rohn, who taught me the importance of doing and becoming better; Brendon Burchard, who taught me how to market everything I do; Michael Sheenan, who taught me the importance of staying on message; Zig Ziglar, who taught me the importance of a regular dose of motivation; Joel Roberts, who taught me the language of impact; and, of course, Robert Anton Wilson, who taught me to look at the same situation from multiple points of view.

Then there are my friends and colleagues. The person I have become is largely a result of the impact that so many of these incredible people have had on me.

Perhaps, though, the greatest influence on me in my life has been my parents, the greatest role models I know. My dad has taught me the value of honesty, kindness, integrity and goodness. He is one of my best friends and the man I look up to the most. My mam is my heart and soul. She has taught me the value of being yourself, loving with all your heart and how to care for others. I could never be loved by anyone more than by those two, nor love anyone more than I love them. They are the greatest people I know and they have done so much for me throughout my life. I haven't always been the best son, but if I do ever have children and could be even half the parent they both are, my children will be blessed. I can't express in words how much they mean to me or how in awe I am of them both. They truly are my greatest influences.

There are many other people who have influenced me powerfully during the course of my life and no doubt there will be more. My mind went back and I remembered particular individuals who made an impression.

With my parents at the launch of my book The Charismatic Edge *in Dublin.*

29. THE ANGELS OF YOUR LIFE

ONE OF THE POPULAR TRENDS in the self-help and spirituality industry in Ireland is the phenomenon of angels. There are many books and workshops on the subject and they have a huge following. What I believe is that, regardless of the question of the existence of angels in a spiritual form, there are such angels in our own lives.

There are some people who just bound into your life and make a real impact on you – a real imprint. As I've mentioned, there are those who are the most important people in your life: your family and friends. There are your business mentors and colleagues. And then there are the people who might have been in your life for just a short while but who changed something in the way you thought and helped your heart when it needed to be helped. I want to talk about three such individuals who made a great difference to me over the years.

When I attended my very first NLP trainings, in the mid-1990s, there were a number of people who would help out on the London courses. One of them was a tall, well-built Polish man in his late forties with a ponytail, who had spent years in Britain. His name was Anton Raps.

Anton was a pleasure to be around. He always spoke his mind. In a world where people too often feel the need to be over-positive, it was wonderful to listen to Anton ranting about this or that, always engaging you, mostly saying things you knew were spot on.

I spent many a pint talking to Anton and to our close mutual friend Steve Tromans. Anton took me under his wing. I was the youngest among us and he was always willing to share his insights on NLP and the mind to help me develop my skills. We soon became friends and I'd search Anton out each day when we'd all arrive at the pub. Anton's words of wisdom were always useful and they never failed to get me thinking. Perhaps one of the most important lessons I got from him was the suggestion to read Robert Anton Wilson.

Having had his work recommended to me a number of times, I had tried to start reading him, but each time I found myself struggling with the nested stories and anecdotes he would impart. When Anton questioned me once about whether or not I had read any of Robert's work I admitted that I hadn't. He then made it clear that if I wasn't prepared to find the gold in Robert's writings I would always be limiting myself.

So, with his prompting, I forced myself to get stuck into two of Robert's books, *Prometheus Rising* and *Quantum Psychology*. I found them to be among the most profoundly powerful books I had ever read. I then read as much of Robert as I could find and he became one of the most important authors to me.

After a few years Anton moved to Thailand and I visited him when I was travelling through that part of the world in January 2006. I remember waiting for him with my backpack in a British pub in the small seaside resort he resided in. Though we hadn't seen each other in years, we started up like normal and tucked into some pub grub as he explained what life was like. Anton was an old-fashioned cynic and he referred to himself as a grump. *Conversations* had been out a few months and he was proud of me for getting it done. We caught up on our lives and discussed philosophy, spirituality, psychology and NLP for hours. It was a wonderful visit.

Anton also repeated what he had told me years ago in what was another significant lesson that I would bring with me in my career. In one of our pub conversations Anton recalled that Richard continually emphasised the importance of state. "State is everything", he said. "Richard does so much work on state because of how important it is. Change your state and you're in the best position to impact others." Once again, it took a stern look from Anton for me to get the message. As I applied the concept, it significantly helped in how effective I was. When I focused more on going into the right emotional state, I found myself getting far better results. I promised myself I would visit him again soon.

It was in 2003 that I met David Northrop. David is someone who had a profound influence on me in the field of NLP. One of the most intelligent people I've ever met, he and I connected while I assisted the NLP trainings in Florida, where David helped out Richard, John and Kathleen (LaValle) every February and March. Even though he didn't do formal NLP training, David was one of the most skilled NLPers I'd ever seen and a brilliant hypnotist.

Of all the assistants I got to know over the years in Orlando, David is the one I connected with most. We spent a lot of time hanging out, going for lunch and dinner together. He would regale me with stories from the computer world, where he worked. I barely understood the jargon, but he had a fantastic way with words. He would come up with the funniest and coolest one-liners. I could never recall them afterwards, but he would remember a host of them and could recount them at will, each one provoking continuous laughter. My continuous laughter.

David was an incredible listener and was always at the other end of an email or phone call in order to help me out with a question I needed resolving. I would ask David for feedback quite a lot and he would always tell it to me straight, but in a caring, compassionate and usually extremely funny way. His refreshing cynicism and considered thinking made it so easy to be around him.

I learnt a lot of valuable skills from David, but I got perhaps the greatest lesson of all the last time I met him, strangely enough also in 2006. In Orlando, David brought me over to the bookshop in the hotel we worked in. It was the day after the trainers' training we'd both been assisting on and I'd asked him to recommend some books to me. Once again, I started talking about my problems and asked what advice he might have for me. "My advice is to start taking your own advice." I looked at him puzzled and he continued, "You look outside of you for the answers to the questions. Now, I'm very happy to help, but unless you start making decisions for yourself you'll never be able to handle what comes your way. You started in this field young. But you're not that kid any more. You've grown up. So you need to be making your own decisions. Stop bitching about who misunderstands you. Handle it."

David's advice cut straight to the matter. My ego didn't want to hear it, but I knew instantly that he was right. That one piece of advice made such an impact on me. It taught me that I needed to start taking full responsibility for the life I would live.

In this world, you will face huge challenges. People will try and knock you off your perch. You will have to handle the naysayers, the begrudgers and the jealous and you're on your own. There will be those who want to see you fall; want to see you fail. You will be misunderstood and people will make up their mind about you in such a way that you'll be stuck reeling from the impact of their confirmation bias. They will see what they expect. And you will have to deal with the politics, deal with the egos and deal with your own.

You might have support, yes. But if you truly want to live the great life, you need to stand up and be your own person. Challenges will come along. Asking for help is a good thing, but real help is that which gives you the ability and perspective to help yourself.

Indeed, to me, that's what the change work we do in the field of NLP is all about. Whether through coaching or therapy, your job is to help your client to be able to stand on their own two feet and to use the skills you teach them to take control over their lives. That warm day in Orlando, a few miles from Universal Studios Florida, I learnt a universal lesson that has changed my life.

I also first met Ron Perry in Orlando, during an NLP seminar I was assisting with. Ron and his wife, Edie, had been long-term students of Richard and had a real expertise in the area of bodywork. Indeed, they created the "patterns of physical transformation".

When I had back trouble I got to experience their healing hands personally. It was obvious why they were considered to be among the best in the world in their field. I remember enjoying many a laugh with Ron. A gentle giant, he would come up with hilarious sayings that always improved the mood of any situation. Whenever I saw him he'd have a cheeky smile and would lovingly tease me in a way that was always funny and always caring.

I learnt a very valuable lesson from my time with Ron: expertise isn't about who shouts the loudest but about who cares the most. Often, Ron was one of the quieter trainers, but was also one of the most respected. He was the kind of guy everybody liked. He never brought an ego into a room, only a warm spirit. For it wasn't just his skills with his hands that helped him heal people: it was the depth of his heart.

Sadly, Ron passed away in August 2012. Many, many people mourned his loss, for it was really our loss. The field of NLP lost a leading light that day. His legacy will live on, however, as that of a great contributor to making the world a better place for so many people. It will live on in the work of his wife, partner, best friend and true love, Edie.

David didn't do NLP training. He liked what he did with computers. But he certainly made a huge difference to me. Heartbreakingly, on 4 November 2008, David passed away suddenly. I found out only much later. When I learned of it I was devestated. Rattled to the core. Sometimes someone can be in your life just a short amount of time, yet they make a huge impact. I will never forget his warmth, his humour and his honesty. He was truly a kindred spirit who I will remember with love for ever.

It was springtime, on Saturday, 31 March 2012, during a course I was teaching in Milan, I was checking my email. The lunchbreak was drawing to an end. I needed to reply to a message regarding my first teaching engagement in Thailand. I was due to travel there that August and needed to get back to them to solidify dates. I was excited and vowed to get in touch with my old friend Anton the next time I was there. I hadn't talked to him in a few years, except for an email at Christmas a couple of years before. I had so much to tell him. My plan was to take some time off before or after the workshop and hang out with him for a few days. Once I had this date nailed down I'd email him straight away. I couldn't wait to catch up on all the news, to fill him in on my life and to find out all about his.

Then, while browsing Facebook, I came across a message that made my heart sink instantly. On my friend Steve's profile I saw the announcement. Anton had passed away. Cancer.

I was devastated. I couldn't believe it. I was going to visit him. I was going to get in touch. I was going to email him . . . one of these days. But I never got to. I never talked to him. I never got the chance.

That afternoon in Milan was one of the most difficult sessions I've ever had to teach. It took every ounce of state-control to stay composed. Then, finally, I left the hotel. I broke down and cried my eyes out. I felt loss and grief and regret – horrible, horrible regret. The same regret I had on hearing the news about David and Ron.

I was supposed to see them again. We were supposed to have a beer together. David was supposed to give me one of his hilarious but genius wise old sayings. We were supposed to go to a diner nearby and joke around about stuff. Anton was supposed to go on one of his beloved rants. These guys were mentors to me, friends to me, there for me. And I didn't even know until it was too late. I found it hard to forgive myself and wished I could turn back the clock. But it was too late.

A few days later Karen, a mutual friend of Anton's and mine, told me about his last few weeks alive. She had spent some time with him as he fought the disease. I told her how bad I felt about not being in touch with him and she replied that she had herself mentioned to him how she had been feeling bad for the same reason. His response was "Don't feel sorry; I don't notice time like that with my friends."

Even as I write his words now, I well up – so beautifully put. I wanted so badly to talk to Anton over chicken-and-chips pub grub, to tell him how I've been getting on, to hear how he's been doing, to get his insights, to make him proud. I wanted so badly to have another trip to the bookshop or the bar with David, to hear his great advice, hilarious jokes and nerdy stories, which seemed to clear up everything I'd been thinking. I wanted so badly to see Ron's glistening smile and hear his smart remarks on some silly mistake I made that make everyone laugh, me most of all. I was supposed to see them again.

But I can't. I can only cherish their memories. In doing so, I must also remember to do my best to appreciate the people I do still have in my life. The people who affect me so much. The people who are my angels. The people who make a difference.

The pain of regretting never saying goodbye is something that stings like hell. But it's got to be a wake-up call. A wake-up call never to let myself take those closest to me for granted. A wake-up call never to assume that one day I'll get a chance to spend time with them. A wake-up call never to forget to appreciate the wonderful experience of loving other people.

There's a fantastic scene at the end of *The Return of the Jedi* in which Luke Skywalker is hugging everyone while the planet celebrates gaining its freedom from Darth Vader and the emperor. Luke looks up and sees a hologram of three figures standing there: his father (Anakin Skywalker) and his two mentors (Obi-Wan Kenobi and Yoda). It symbolises the belief that those that pass from this world are looking down upon us and watching over us. It's how I see things.

Tragically, this isn't the end of the story. Just the other day, I learned more devestating news. My friend Jeff Schoener who assisted on many of the trainings with me in Orlando died suddenly.

Jeff and his wife Natalie were a beautiful example of a couple destined to be with each other. Introduced by friends, they first talked on the phone and instantly hit it off. I remember the last time the three of us had dinner hearing about the story. As they told me, you could see the absolute love in their eyes. In a world filled with billions of people and they found each other.

The thing with Jeff is that he isn't the kind of guy that will be out and out smiley or in your face friendly. He's friendly but in his own way. It took me a little time to get to really know him but once I did, I really got him. Jeff didn't just agree with you for the sake of it. He agreed and he challenged, his brain always on. Besides his smarts and his skill, his biggest strength was his heart. He really did care for people so much and was a real giver.

The biggest lesson I learned from Jeff was in who he was. He was a great example of someone who used the skills of NLP on himself and then applied them to others in a caring and effective way. He didn't spend time marketing how good he was like some of us do. He was just amazing and, with his quiet presence, he made a huge difference to so many people. Because he cared.

The final time we assisted together, myself and Jeff hung out more than usual. We ran one of the stations together in the DHE course with the *Star Wars* mind power equipment.

When the machines weren't working, we improvised and together entertained the crowds as they waited in line. We messed around with toy lightsabers. We had a super laugh. Jeff showed me some of the fantastic work he was doing with an app he had developed for giving yourself suggestions more effectively. We talked about NLP, the past and the future. We talked about the future.

When I met Jeff and Natalie a month later in New York we had a lovely sunday lunch in a kosher restaraunt. We had a great chat and a laugh and I said goodbye to them at the corner of the street afterward. If I had that moment back I'd tell him that I love him and how impressed I am with who he is and how much he has done. I'd tell him how amazing a person he is. I'd tell him all the things that I want him to know. The pain in my heart reveals just how much he meant to me. I was driving and had to pull over when I heard the news about Jeff. Once again, I felt sick. Once again, I felt a sharp pang of pain and the tears began. Once again, a beautiful friend was taken from my life.

Jeff, Ron, Anton, David. Four incredible souls. Four incredible spirits. They left a gap in my life. Of course, there are people that they leave behind. Their wives and families. Amazing women like Edie and Natalie. My heart hopes that they each continue to have the strength to move on day-by-day, year-by-year despite the heartbreak of losing an incredible man.

They are not the only great men I knew in NLP that have passed on. John Brown (Brownie) is another wonderful friend that passed before his time. An infectious laugh, bright smile and a face like Santa will always keep Brownie in my thoughts. His great hypnotic skills and real impact on me has never been forgotten.

These men remain with us in the memories we have. People may pass on from this world. But as they do, they leave their own mark on the planet and the people in it. They left their mark on me and I will never be the same because of it. The lessons I learnt will never be forgotten and those wonderful men will have a place in my heart for ever. Gone, but never forgotten.

30. THE RICHEST PERSON EVER TO HAVE LIVED

IT'S PRETTY MUCH IMPOSSIBLE to read a newspaper or watch television without somebody, somewhere, telling us how screwed we are. The financial crisis, as they call it, is the greatest thing to have happened to the media since the War on Terror. It's the perfect story: terrifying, real, relevant and ever present.

So, the world has changed quite significantly over the past few years and we've been forced into dealing with it. We're told that money can make us happier. We're told that we have to accept the fact that we won't make as much money as before. We're told that, any minute now, things could get even worse.

It's like a horror movie that keeps going on and on and on, with no end in sight. Throughout the world there has been massive outrage. The politicians and bankers are the enemies and face a constant public backlash. The money is gone and they screwed the whole thing up.

At the same time, everyone still wants to be rich. Wealth itself is an industry. There are many who are getting rich teaching others how to be rich. "Invest $1,000 and you will learn how you can make $50,000 a month." Promises. Offers. Apparent opportunities.

In a world where we recently forgot that money is a finite resource and ended up in great difficulties as a result, we now seem to be more desperate than ever. Happiness is being trumped by cold, hard cash. And yet, the truth is that we're failing to look past the surface.

The truth is that the richest people I know are the ones with the best memories. On your deathbed the only things that will matter will be the people around you and the memories of your life. Your cash won't help you feel better; your possessions won't comfort you. It will be the memories that have made your life worthwhile and filled you with meaning that will be most important.

The moment you leave this world you will do so only with memories. They are the images of your past, a reminder of the events of your life. When you die you will take them to your grave, eternally. We all have them. Good ones, bad ones, happy ones, sad ones. They remind you of how great things were and how horrible things were. They show you lessons that you learn and some that you never seem to learn.

Your life is packed full of experiences and these experiences become your memories. Sometimes you forget them and sometimes you remember them differently from how they actually happened. Sometimes hindsight means you think about the past very differently because of how things have eventually transpired.

Your memories are precious. They help create the foundation of your identity, of who you think you are. They can become your greatest source of inspiration and your biggest source of pain. We all have things in our lives we can't remember and those we can't forget. Unfortunately, many of the things we can't forget we wish we would and many of things we can't remember we wish we could. Nostalgia sometimes acts as a dangerous temptress lulling us into a false sense of dissatisfaction with the present day. Our brains can make yesteryear seem like paradise as it filters out the reality checks and balances of such a time.

The uncertainty of the future and the challenges of the present often prompt us to revert to the past – the experiences we know and feel comfortable with, the certainty of what is known and understood. We draw security from the memories of our lives and our ability to remember helps us feel grounded and safe.

Occasionally our memories can do the opposite. Our fears, stresses, worries and insecurities are largely a product of the way we think about our past experiences. We have had challenges or feelings of stress and terror in our lives before and we concern ourselves with the future replicating the past. We are continuously running away from or towards the past. Meanwhile, our present is disappearing, adding to our past. We are failing to truly live.

We have certain memories that are painful and tragic and others that put a gigantic smile on our face. Memories, you see, are one of the most important elements of our thoughts. They are what makes us who we are. How we deal with them also determines how we live our life. We can be ruined by memories, or they can inspire us. But one thing is for sure: how we allow them to affect us will determine how we lead our lives.

The last thing you will ever own is also the most important. When we ask ourselves the ultimate question, was my life worth it?, our memories will dictate the answer. What you are about to read is not just a collection of our memories: it is a set of ideas for ensuring that you can create the best kind of memories by creating the best kind of moments in your life – the moments that have become the memories of our lives.

31. MEMORIES FOR TOMORROW

WHEN WE BEGAN WRITING THIS BOOK I knew that one of the most important things our experiences provide is perspective. Working on it has been in many ways a remarkable opportunity for extracting learnings and understandings from my life and from Richard's life. Looking at your life differently makes a huge difference to how you actually live.

Because I began in this field when I was just a teenager, my memories largely consist of experiences filtered through my NLP worldview. I still remember my very first workshop with Richard, when I found myself laughing so hard that my face was really sore afterwards. I realised that my life was missing something. Back then, having been depressed and suicidal, I had been living a life full of misery, because I simply didn't know it was possible to change my future.

I remember thinking, maybe NLP will allow me to create a new life; maybe I can turn things around. It was the beginning of hope for a better future. People would always tell me how I was so lucky to have learnt NLP early on in life. They'd say, "If only I knew this stuff when I was your age. . ." But the reality was often that you could meet the same people seven years on and things weren't much different for them.

The truth is that it's not NLP that will change your life: it's what you do. Early on in my career I went through a number of different stages. What was true in each stage was that I was obsessed with and focused on, applying everything I had learnt over and over again. Regardless of what I was going through, I was always dedicated to becoming as skilful as possible and to being in as much control over my mind as possible. I worked really hard and still do, to improve the language I use and in my ability to understand and help people.

The reason my life changed was that I changed. But not in who I was, because I believe that we are all the very best versions of ourselves. I believe I changed how I thought, what I believed, how I behaved, what I did and, of course, how I felt. Life throws challenges your way and you must be able to dig deep and find a way through them, to learn how to grow from them. It's a choice we talked about in *Conversations* and making such a choice has tremendous power.

As I contemplated my future, I began to look forward to all that would be in store for me. There were so many things that hadn't happened yet but that I believed would. People I hadn't met yet. Experiences I hadn't had yet. Adventures I hadn't gone on yet. The future was full of memories I hadn't yet made. I wanted to hear from Richard on the subject of what he believed about the future and the memories that are yet to exist.

    OF: Richard, could you talk to us about future memories?
    RB: When we talk about future memories it's the old question that everybody asks: "Where is NLP going?" Which is really asking, "What am I going to do next?" The answer to that is really quite simple. When I started out, years and years and years ago, while I was labelled a Gestalt therapist, or labelled a musician, or labelled an undergraduate, my background and my first degree was in philosophy. I studied symbolic logic. I studied any philosopher who talked about epistemological things, that is, the study of knowledge. How do we think?

And you can't talk about how we think unless you talk about the machine that does it.

Neurology, neurochemistry – all of these fields are blossoming right now. Our understanding of how the brain works and doesn't work, is increasing all the time. We're learning things about biochemistry and we're learning things about the universe that we never knew – that a lot of the things that were theories Einstein had are now being found in fact: our view of the world, which is connected to our senses . . . And those things extend our senses – all the devices we use to measure light and sound and the telescopes, like the Hubble Space Telescope that looks across the vast universe in which we live. The more we study suns that are light years away and find out what they're made of, the more we see that, in reality, you have two choices: you can go, "How different is this?" or you can say, "Where are the similarities?"

When I started out, the first thing I did was look at what great, "successful" psychotherapists had in common – Virginia Satir, Milton Erickson, some people who are not famous. But the people who got results – not all the time, but when they got results – had to all be doing the same thing. They were affecting learning. They were changing the knowledge in the brain so that it changed the way people felt and changed what they could do and changed the quality of their experience.

Even as an undergraduate I worked in schools. It wasn't because my goal was to become a psychotherapist. When I worked with learning-disabled kids I didn't look for the answer in the teaching methods that were being used: I looked for the answer in the people who could successfully do the behaviours. When they told me a kid was learning-disabled, there was nothing to me that was different to this kid than anybody else, except that they couldn't do certain things. And I would get a list. I'd go, "What can't they do?" and they'd go, "They have a short attention span." And I could only sympathise with them, having been to school, because I could see where your attention span would run out!

The answer didn't lie in the learning-disabled kid but in finding out if they couldn't spell. You go and get good spellers and find out how they did it. With psychotherapists, the answer really wasn't in studying what good psychotherapists did. The answer was somewhere else. And really where neuro-linguistic programming achieved being a field and did something interesting is when we stopped looking at the skills that were out there but instead used those skills – the language patterns and all of those things – to start finding out how successful people did things. You could study thousands of depressives and find out how they got that way and how their neurochemistry is out, but the question is: How do you think differently to become a happier person?

If all you studied was insomniacs, then you could develop a model to teach people how to stay awake. But if you want to get people to sleep better, deeper and be healthier, then you have to study people to sleep deeper and get healthier and find out what they do and teach other people to do it. If somebody plays basketball well and ten other people can't shoot well, you don't study the people who shoot badly to find out what they're doing wrong. You study the people that are doing well and teach the other people to use the same thought patterns.

I remember seeing a Goofy cartoon – a Disney cartoon – where Goofy was playing pool and he visualised lines on the table so he would know where to hit the ball – to adjust the geometry so that he could knock it off of one bank and hit another one and hit the ball in. I remember sitting there and thinking to myself for the first time, I kind of understood what a pool-player did. To me, I never had that much interest in pool, but suddenly it became more interesting, because there was something you could do to become a better pool-player. Over the years, we've developed techniques, technology, skills, so that we can begin to look at things.

Now, what am I going to look at next? I don't know. But I can guarantee you it will be successful people. Just like I looked at Milton [Erickson] and Virginia [Satir] and Moshé [Feldenkrais] when it came to bodywork. There are lots of people who are stuck in various levels of my development and bragging about whether they had something to do with its creation. I've got no interest in that, myself. I want to know what's next! And what's next is that there are loads of other bright people out there, whether it's discovering how an architect thinks or how somebody does whatever better.

I've worked with great athletes. I've worked with successful businesspeople. I made a series of films that are just about success in London recently. It's time to begin to go to the source of successful behaviours across the board. And I'm sure there are going to be other smart, genius people that I'll meet along the way. And the skills that I have are about modelling those.

We need to build a better educational system in every country in this world. It's time for us to stop fooling around, thinking that we can get education to be better because we can throw more money at it. If you're doing the same thing it doesn't matter how much money you spend on it. It's not about whether there's fifteen kids in a class or thirty: it's about the presentation of the skills and teaching them to love learning. Our school systems are designed so that very few people really enjoy the process of learning mathematics. We need to build lots of scientists. We're at the frontier of probably the greatest century that ever was.

They asked in a magazine that I read recently, "Where will computers be in 150 years? In 50 years? 100 years?" And all the top brain computer people all said, "I have no idea. None whatsoever." They couldn't even imagine where computers would be in a hundred years, or memory systems and what they'll be able to do. Many of the things that are science fiction at one time have become real. There was science fiction of being in a submarine under the water and now there are submarines floating all over the ocean. They're so big they're unbelievable when you go inside, some of these military things! You look at the size of cruise ships – a hundred years ago people would have thought that it didn't even come from this planet. Knowledge is increasing exponentially, not mathematically. Everything is going faster, because we're thinking faster. We're exposed to more information. We're being exposed to media, to the web – all of these things that didn't exist.

Recently, I told my grandson I was thinking of buying him a set of encyclopaedias, to which his response was "Isn't that kind of old school?" So instead I got him a computer – set him up with an iMac so that he could go on and search any subject about anything. Unfortunately, the knowledge on the web, unlike encyclopaedias, is not double-checked. So not only do we have to have people gaining knowledge, we have to have people who are more discerning about it. We have to teach people to have better judgement. I've read over a dozen people claiming to have made up the term "neuro-linguistic programming", which is ludicrous. I know where it came from: I made it up. I know where I was when I made it up. And yet when you go on the web all this stuff is out there.

Now, it's a good thing that there's lots of versions of everything available, but we all have to have the ability to go back to the source. I didn't learn hypnosis from one of Milton's students. I went to the source. If I want to learn about nuclear physics, I want to go to somebody that's built a nuclear power plant, that's done work in nuclear physics. If I want to learn about astronomy, I want to talk to somebody who's actually seen things through the Hubble Space Telescope. If I want to learn about string theory, I want somebody that's actually done something with it, not just somebody that talks about it. There are people that have actually built things so that, for example, you can charge your cell phone by using the fact that weak energy moves through a forcefield as the Earth turns!

To me, always making a distinction between the people that do and the people that describe is really important. The more I find people that can do things, the more I'll be able to find out how they're thinking to be able to do those things. Whether it's an accounting course or spelling in school, not only do we have to teach them how it functions, we have to teach them how they can think. The NLP spelling strategy still isn't being used in most schools. The fact that visualising a word that's twelve inches – as opposed to one the size of a typewritten page – is easier to read isn't rocket science. Yet all these textbooks being provided by the schools don't teach kids the mental capability that they need to perform a task. They need to be able to say to themselves, wow! I did this!

There was tremendous resistance to calculators when they first were invented. I remember, even though calculators were three hundred dollars, I bought my son one. When he took it to school they got angry at him. They said, "It's cheating. Not everybody has one." And when I contacted the manufacturer they sent me a big box of them so that I could hand them out. They still didn't want kids to use them, because they said if you use a calculator you'll never learn to add. That's not really true!

The truth is that when you learn to use the newest machines, the newest in technology, you benefit the most! A lot of people say it's wrong that kids are sitting with their cell phones, searching the web. What's wrong is that we haven't taught them to search for great things. They're not exploring the limits of science. They may be gaming, but at least the games are teaching them to be able to fantasise reality and make it real.

All creation in all science is where you imagine a possibility and you build it. At one time there were no cars. People imagined them. Now they're everywhere. People are still improving upon the automobile constantly. They get better gas mileage, better aerodynamics. Especially when it comes to our educational system, we should have the same kind of mental engineering that we have in physical engineering if we're ever going to get to the stars and if we're ever going to be able to evolve whatever it takes.

We don't know how fast we'll ultimately be able to travel, or whether we'll make doors that cut through space, or whether we'll have to travel for generations to get somewhere and travel for generations to get back. And whether we'll evolve by nature. Evolution will take over. If we spend generations in space our blood chemistry will change. We've evolved and adapted to the environments we were in on Planet Earth. The one thing about successful organisms is their adaptability.

To me, when I look to the future, I look to new challenges, tougher things to try, things to improve the technology that we've already created – and looking to neurology and to science and to those special people that have that "can do" spirit to find out new things that can be done.

Now, I have lots of students that talk a good game, but there is really a very small number of them that have that can-do spirit. It's one thing to overcome a difficulty; it's another to charge towards a horizon. To me, I'm looking for those special individuals that are like me, charging towards the horizon, saying, "I don't care how hard it is. I don't care how tough it is. We can all do it and we will."

Giving up on clients is the real thing that annoyed me about psychotherapy. When they said that people were immature, or people were resistant, all of these things were excuses not to develop new techniques that work better. We took a bunch of phobics and we figured out how to get them to not be phobics so that they could walk in their closets or walk up an escalator in twenty minutes rather than spending five years whining about where it came from. The best thing about the past is that it's over and the best thing about the future is that it's on its way.

This book is about recalling things. To me, that's all well and good: looking backwards is one thing and it's fun. However, it's a lot more fun to look into the future and realise that all limitations exist in the way we think about things – not in the things themselves.

Those limitations Richard mentioned were the very ones I had overcome in my past. As I looked at the future I began to imagine meeting that someone special, having children and taking care of a family. I began to imagine even more of my ambitions coming true. I began to see myself sharing my ideas and perspectives with many more people throughout the world. I began to see myself building greater connections with more people, building more friendships and enjoying the ones I have even more. I began to see myself creating more ideas that help people in unique ways, that help people learn and transform.

Many of my friends already have partners and children. Some of them have already become ridiculously successful. They've already done things I have yet to do. But there is still so much more out there – so many more wonderful memories and experiences where you can enjoy letting what happens happen, as well as making things happen.

For, you see, as I reflect on my life so far, I realise that this is what I'm here for. It's what we're all here for: to impact the world and to allow the world to impact you. Your future isn't written yet, so the choices you make today will determine the quality of your future memories. The possibilities are so exciting. The opportunities abound. The trick is to allow the tough experiences to make you tougher and wiser and to appreciate the good times as fully as you can.

32. RANDOM RAMBLINGS: THE MOST BEAUTIFUL PLACE ON EARTH

SIXTY THOUSAND SCARVES HELD ALOFT. Green and white everywhere. "You'll Never Walk Alone" belting out of every mouth. Tears streaming down so many faces. Tears of joy. Tears of beauty. Tears of love. Another match: Celtic against FC Barcelona in the European Champions' League. We stole a victory, 2-1. A fairytale result against one of the greatest teams the world has ever known. And I was there. *I was there.*

Despite the things I'm yet to do, I'm extremely lucky to have experienced what I've experienced. I've been on more than my fair share of adventures and I've seen some incredible things. I have met Indian gurus and South American shamans, partied in Las Vegas, explored the Amazon jungle, have been threatened by Central American drug dealers, have got into a number of road accidents and have been chased through the streets of Iran and I have even found myself in Afghanistan and North Korea! I've pushed myself into experiences that challenged me so that I could grow more, become more.

What inspired me to do all this was Richard's wonderful advice: "Do as many different things with as many different people in as many different places as you can."

But I've also seen some incredible things. I've visited the Great Wall of China, the ancient city of Petra in Jordan, the hidden remains of Machu Picchu. I have experienced the Taj Mahal in India, Angkor Wat in Cambodia, the beautiful Japanese gardens on Kyoto, the wonderful volcano near Santorini in Greece, Lake Como in Italy, the wildlife of Africa, the stunning Andes mountains in Peru, the pyramids of Egypt, the spellbinding forests of Guatemala, the serene beauty of the nature of New Zealand and the green, green grass of my beautiful home, Ireland. I've witnessed some of the most marvellous sunsets imaginable and watched the sunrise in every beautiful continent. And, of course, I've seen my beloved Glasgow Celtic and thousands of fans singing in unison for the greatest team on Earth.

But none of this can be compared to my seeing my two god-daughters. From the moment they were born I've felt an incomparable bond with both of them. It's obviously a sense of love and yet it's somehow deeper. Although I don't know yet what it's like to be a father, this gives me some idea, for the most beautiful part of living on this planet is the people you love.

You can go anywhere, but you will always be at home when the right people are there. I can be bored talking about the most interesting subject if I'm with people I don't connect with; I can be excited sitting in silence with someone I do connect with. The beauty of love in this world makes so much of every challenge bearable and so much of every terrific time blissful.

Life can be pretty tough sometimes, especially when someone you love is taken from you. It can be a betrayal, if they find themselves in the arms of another, or it can be because of circumstances whereby you find yourself on the other side of the world. Or it can be a tragedy, where you lose them to fate and find yourself without them.

But that's exactly why it's so important to make every second count with the ones you love.

Whether it's playing with your son or daughter or having tea with your granny, these moments are so precious. For in the time you have available to you in this world, the most important thing you can do is to enjoy the time you spend with your loved ones and to do what you can to connect with more people so that you can find more loved ones.

A few years ago I taught a seminar called "The Art of Happiness" on the island of Okinawa. Although Japan doesn't tend to fare well in the national happiness ratings for the average person, most of the people in Okinawa tend to be extremely happy and live longer lives than in any other place on Earth. There's a saying there: "Ichariba chode" ("Though we meet just once, we are family, or friends, for life"). It seems that love and friendship are highly decisive factors for a happy life.

In Quito that Saturday back in February 2006, after my incredible encounter with ayahuasca and the shamans, with the evening approaching and the experience beginning to subside, it was time to go home. The sun was setting and we had an hour's drive back into the city. I said goodbye to the principal shaman. It was time to start tuning back in to where I was and where we were now going. I approached him and he smiled as he put his hand on my shoulder. His crystal clear eyes looked into mine, into my mind and said, pausing after each word "You . . . came . . . a . . . stranger; you . . . leave . . . my . . . brother". To this day, the hairs on the back of my neck stand up when I remember this and feel that true connection with another human being.

It's one of the beautiful aspects of life that you can create such a connection with a total stranger and that this connection can grow so that they really affect your life. They become your "brothers" or "sisters" and you feel your family of friends growing.

Some of my friends feel at home in nature; others feel at home with their pets. But it's all the same. It's a connection with something that's alive. It's another form of love.

So, for me, the most beautiful time on Planet Earth is when I'm with either of my god-daughters, Lucy or Aoife. It's when I'm with my mother and father, my sister, my uncle, my cousins and my incredible friends. It resides in the best memories of the angels of my life – people like Jeff, David, Anton and Ron – or in my conversations with Richard. It's when I'm with strangers I connect with, surrounded by beautiful nature. Doing what I'm passionate about. Surrounded by life. Surrounded by love. And, of course, Glasgow Celtic.

CONCLUSION: THE PROMISE OF HOPE

THE STORIES WE READ, watch and hear usually centre on the importance of one quality in particular: hope. When the world seems doomed because of bad guys, we look to Superman, Batman, Spiderman, Jack Bauer or James Bond to save the day. They represent our hope that the day will be saved.

When we watch a movie in which two people in love break up, we want them to discover what we all know: that they're supposed to be together. That discovery represents our hope that they will find each other again.

When someone finds themselves in an impossible situation, having been knocked down by life, we look to the insight they need in order to make a change and overcome the challenges they face. This insight represents our hope that they will triumph over adversity. We hope in people. We hope in discoveries. We hope in insights. Hope carries us through. It ignites in us the belief that things can get better.

When I was born on 8 July 1978 in the Coombe Hospital in Dublin, it was the day that Björn Borg won Wimbledon again. My mother actually considered naming me Björn. Thank God she didn't: I was to be bullied anyway, but if I was named Björn in Dublin I would have been a really easy target!

They did manage to get me with my middle name though. I was named Jude, after the patron saint of hopeless cases. At the time it made sense, because I was pretty sick the first few days of my life. Apparently I was put in intensive care. My mum says I fought my way into this world. But hopeless cases? Give me a break.

In the Christian faith, St Jude gives hope to those who have none. A few years ago Richard said something that stayed with me: "Many people think hope is the answer to their problems. In reality, hope is the question." To the challenges of life, to the difficulties we face, to the suffering we encounter. You ask the question and it will lead you to the answers you need.

One of my final questions to Richard centred on the concept of hope.

> OF: What's the importance of hope in the modern world, Richard?
> RB: Well, there are two kinds of hope: there's the kind where you sure hope something good will happen and then there's the kind where you're so hopeful that you know something's going to happen and you're searching with every fibre of your soul to find out what it is. And, to me, one of those is really useful. It's kind of like, you can wish on one hand and shit in the other, but if you smack yourself in the face, only one sticks.

Nicely put – the image stuck! Action is absolutely critical, for hope without action is pointless. Hope with action changes the world. I also realised that it wasn't just hope itself that was important but the strength of your belief that the future can be better, brighter and more brilliant than you can possibly imagine.

I tapped *stop* on my iPhone, put it back in my pocket and thanked Richard. We chatted for a while about the book and about projects Richard had going on.

Then we moved on to talking about Ireland. I reached back into my pocket and took out my recorder again. I had one final question.

> OF: Have you any lasting memories from my beautiful country, Ireland?
>
> RB: Oh, Ireland? Loads of them. I loved living in Ireland. My cottage by the sea was my fortress of solitude, so to speak. It's a very magical place and very magical things happen. I remember this fox coming by the back of my house – this ratty-looking old fox – and it would come by and since I didn't try to bother it or do anything, it kept coming by. Then one day it showed up and it had three little tiny pups.
>
> I had the same experience with Irish hares, which are the biggest rabbits I'd ever seen! One used to come by and I'd look at it out the window, but I didn't pay any attention to it. One day it just came up and stared through the window. It literally put its nose up on the glass and just looked and, rather than get up or move or do anything, I just looked at it out of the corner of my eye and kept watching TV. Somewhere along the line the rabbit decided I wasn't a threat and she brought by little bunnies. I couldn't even give them anything they would eat – I'd given them carrots and stuff – but they just wanted the warmth of the slate in the back of the house.
>
> One day I had the door open and I was talking to Paul McKenna. I remember we were having a conversation and I turned and looked and there were three little tiny bunnies staring in the window.
>
> There was always something like that. Beautiful sunsets and wonderful people. It was a great place to live when I lived there. It's a great country, but it needs a heater.

I laughed. I couldn't have said it better myself.

> OF: Yeah, absolutely. Well, Richard, I want to say thanks for the memories both past and future.
>
> RB: You bet.

No sooner did this conversation end than I was already looking forward to many more conversations and many more chats with Richard over the next few years. For now, we had completed another voyage. This voyage explored our past experiences and revealed many messages and lessons – many insights and perspectives that can help you live a happier and smarter life.

History is full of stories of people who have overcome great challenges. Indeed, the words "story" and "history" are the same in Italian, French and Spanish. Stories teach us valuable insights about the world. They give us perspective. The more perspective we have, the smarter we are. To live happily ever after and smarter ever after, you need to allow yourself to be okay with being wrong and to learn as much as you can.

Memories make life wonderful. Your life will involve people coming and going. Some will be there for long periods and some for just a while. Some will hurt you. Some will help you. Some will make your life hell. Some will make you feel like you're in heaven. Some you won't even remember. Some will truly have an impact on you.

Conclusion

But the beauty is that those who hurt you and make your life hell are there to help you grow stronger and tougher and more able to become better than ever. Those who help you, love you and make you feel like you're in heaven are there to affect you and make you feel more wonderful than ever about your life.

The memories Richard and I discussed got me to understand him more deeply, as well as what drove him to accomplish all he had over the years. They got me to understand myself more deeply as well.

I hope that, as well as having gained further insights into how to cope with a crisis or with the recession, into how to be better in your relationships and into finding ways to change how you communicate, you have taken from this book the most important message of all: the future is full of memories you haven't yet had.

But you have a choice. You have a choice in what kind of memories you create. Not all of them, of course, but far more than you could possibly imagine. It's up to you. It's your time. It's time to build the kind of future you desire. It's time to make the decisions that help you grow and learn and improve. It's time to embrace uncertainty and challenge and to find inside you the strength to overcome. It's time to live the life you were born to live.

How do you want to be known? What do you want to be known for? What do you want your final memories to be? What is most important to you? These questions are fundamental questions, for they get us to connect with a greater part of ourselves. They get us to really understand ourselves.

More than forty years ago Richard began to model some of the most successful therapists of all time. The theories he jointly established in the 1970s have transformed the field of personal change. The insights gained have revolutionised the industry. Psychologists are finally catching up with the ideas proposed. But there is still a bit to go in understanding what influenced Richard to do what he did, in understanding where the ideas came from, in understanding how to think more effectively about the challenges and uncertainty of modern society, in understanding how to improve our relationships and families, in understanding the importance of thinking at a level higher than a spiritual perspective. We learn one fundamental insight throughout all those perspectives: the importance of hope.

My life has had its fair share of challenges. I've had my ups and downs, my good times and bad times. I have my memories of people in my life who I will never forget. And they all made an impact on me. There will be more.

To me, again, that's what life is all about. Two things: making an impact on the world and allowing the world to make an impact on you. Allow life to touch you, inspire you, even hurt you and allow that hurt to be transformed into strength. Make sure that you too make an impact. A real impact. An impact that lasts. An impact that matters. An impact that changes the world for the better.

As we spin around on this blue and green ball that is the Earth, we face an uncertain future. But we must rise up and see this in a new way. We're more capable than we have ever been. We have accomplished incredible feats, amazing endeavours. And we aren't finished yet. We must remember what we've done and what we can do. We need to create that movement towards a better life and heal the planet by making better decisions in our own lives. To attain true happiness, we must learn to appreciate what we have and feel good about moving towards what we want. We must learn to swim. Therein lies the balance.

Sometimes memories never fade; sometimes they last for ever. My granny seemed to remember her late son, Tony, throughout her illness. She was very religious and knew that she would finally see him again in heaven when she passed on.

Some time before she died, her other son, my uncle Shay, brought her the census form in order that she would sign her name and mark the date so that the local community would have her officially registered. Instead of signing her own name she clearly signed that of her deceased son, Tony O'Neill. She dated it 16 June 2012. My Uncle Shay corrected her and said, "No, your name, mam and today's date is in January." She simply smiled at him. Granny was buried on 16 June 2012.

I will remember my granny for ever. I will remember all my other loved ones who have passed on. My friends, my other family members – I will remember them all and they will always exist in my heart. And they will make my heart stronger and more full of love. The future awaits and it's exciting. It's exciting because there's so much more to learn, so much more to do, so much more to experience, so many more memories to build.

When I close my eyes I can imagine a better future. I can see all that I want in it and I believe it's all possible. But that's not enough. All my memories were created by what I did in my life, so that's the most important part. Once you have hope and perspective, you do get smarter and if you're smart enough to take action, the world will work out for you. For in the face of the boldness of intelligent action, challenges step aside and possibilities unfold. It's exciting. And whatever you've been through, however many times you've tried and not yet succeeded, today is the day you get a fresh beginning. Today is the day to really live.

When you close the final page of this book, make it count. Create the kind of memories that will make your life incredible. Create the kind of beliefs that empower you. Create a sense of hope for your future. This is your time to claim the kind of life you want. You have the tools. You have the perspectives. You have all you need to think differently. The question is: Will you? Will you do what it takes? Will you commit to enjoying your life more? Will you remind yourself of the fundamental truth that it is love that makes life worthwhile? It is love that helps you handle anything. And it is love that, fundamentally, changes the world.

ACKNOWLEDGEMENTS

From both of us:

John and Kathleen LaValle, wonderful friends who have been an amazing support over the years.

Our clients and students over the years who have taught us so much about so much.

From Owen:

My family for being everything to me.

My friends, far too many to mention, for making my memories so full of love.

My two cousins Breandan Kearney and Donal Kearney and my friend Paul Kiernan who helped specifically with this book with reading, transcribing and editing.

Gillian McNamara Fowley and Sandra Pou Van Biezen for reading this in advance and for all the other amazing help you give me.

Paddy O'Shea for helping me promote this book to the world.

Brian Colbert and Theresa Colbert. Fantastic friends and colleagues I am lucky to work with.

To Adrienne Foran and the great team at Brunswick Press for making this happen.

To Don Harper. A fantastic help with the book and a great professional.

Thanks to Ruairí O Brógáin and Antoinette Walker for copy editing and proofreading with short notice.

To Alessio Roberti and Kate Benson for all their support and help.

GLOSSARY OF TERMS

Below is a list of some of the main processes related to NLP that are discussed in this book.

Anchoring
The process of associating an internal response with an external trigger, so that the response can be reaccessed.

Auditory
Relating to the sense of hearing.

Behaviour
The specific actions we take.

Calibration
The process of learning to read another person's unconscious, non-verbal responses, by observing another's behaviour and the relation of their behaviour with their internal response.

Congruence
When a person's beliefs, state and behaviour are all fully oriented towards securing a desired outcome.

Conscious Mind
The part of your mind that is working when you are alert and aware. It is your critical faculty and your source of reason and logic. It seems to run constantly all day while you are awake and its focus is always on particular thoughts. It is mainly controlled by the automatic processes of the unconscious mind.

Criteria
The values a person uses to make decisions.

Design Human Engineering®
A technology and evolutionary tool created by Dr Bandler in the late 1980s–early 1990s which focuses on using more of our brain to do more than was previously possible.

Gustatory
Relating to the sense of taste.

Hypnosis
An application of NLP as well as a field in its own right. Hypnosis is the process of guiding a person into a state where they have more direct access to their unconscious mind which is where powerful changes can be made, deliberately through the use of suggestion.

Kinesthetic
Related to body sensations.

Magic
The art of creating an illusion.

Glossary

Magick
The art of using natural forces to bring about change. Often associated with the occult.

Meta-Model
A model developed by Richard Bandler and John Grinder that suggests questions which enable people to specify information, clarify information and open up and enrich the model of a person's world.

Meta Program
A learned process for sorting and organising information and internal strategies.

Metaphor
Stories and analogies.

Milton Model
A model developed by Richard Bandler and John Grinder on the patterns of hypnotic techniques used by Milton H. Erickson, the clinical hypnotherapist and other masters of persuasion.

Neuro-Hypnotic Repatterning™
A technology which uses the hypnotic process to restructure people at the level of cortical pathways.

Neuro-Linguistic Programming
An attitude, methodology and technology which teaches people how to improve the quality of their lives. It is an educational tool which teaches people how to communicate more effectively with themselves and with others. It is designed to help people to have personal freedom in the way they think, feel and behave.

Rapport
The existence of trust and harmony in a relationship.

Representational Systems
The five systems that we take information in from the world. Through these systems (our five senses) we create a representation of the information we take in.

Sleight of Mouth Patterns
A set of language patterns that helps you challenge limiting beliefs. In particular, beliefs that are framed as X causes Y or X means Y.

State
The total ongoing mental, emotional and physical conditions of a person at a given moment of time.

Strategy
A set of mental and behavioural steps to achieve an outcome.

Sub-Modalities
The sensory qualities of the representations we create through our representational systems.

Trance
A state commonly experienced as a result of hypnosis. It is also a state of mind that is characterised by a focus of thought. We live in many different trances depending on what our mind is absorbed in at any given moment (television, driving, eating, etc.).

Unconscious Installation
The process of installing skills, ideas and suggestions inside a person through communicating with their unconscious mind.

Unconscious Mind
The part of your mind that is working all the time. It is what produces your dreams and regulates your bodily functions such as your heartbeat, breathing and habitual patterns of behaviour. It contains all your memories, wisdom and perception. It runs the automatic programmes of thinking and behaving and therefore is the best place to make changes permanent.

Well-Formed Outcomes
Goals that are set according to well-formed conditions. These conditions are that the goals must be positive, specific, sensory based, ecological and maintainable by the individual themselves.

Visual
Relating to the sense of sight.

RECOMMENDED READING

Bandler, Richard, *Using Your Brain for a Change*, Real People Press, Durango, CO, 1985
— , *Magic in Action*, Meta Publications, Capitola, CA, 1985
— , *The Adventures of Anybody*, Meta Publications, Capitola, CA, 1993
— , *Time for a Change*, Meta Publications, Capitola, CA, 1993
— , *Get the Life You Want*, HarperElement, London, 2008
— , *Make Your Life Great*, HarperElement, London, 2010
Bandler, Richard, Delozier, Judith and Grinder, John, *Patterns of the Hypnotic Techniques of Milton H. Erickson*, Volume 2, Meta Publications, Capitola, CA, 1977
Bandler, Richard and Grinder, John, *Frogs into Princes*, Real People Press, Capitola, CA, 1979
— , Patterns of the Hypnotic Techniques of Milton H. *Erickson*, Volume 1, Meta Publications, Capitola, CA, 1975
— , *The Structure of Magic*, Meta Publications, Capitola, CA, 1975
— , *The Structure of Magic*, Volume 2, Meta Publications, Capitola, CA, 1975
— , *Trance-formations*, Real People Press, Durango, CO, 1980
Bandler, Richard and Fitzpatrick, Owen, *Conversations with Richard Bandler*, Health Communications, Deerfield Beach, FL, 2009
Bandler, Richard and LaValle, John, *Persuasion Engineering*, Meta Publications, Capitola, CA, 1996
Bandler, Richard and McDonald, Will, *An Insider's Guide to Submodalities*, Meta Publications, Capitola, CA, 1989
Bandler, Richard, Roberti, Alessio and Fitzpatrick, Owen, *How to Take Charge of Your Life: The Users Guide to NLP*, HarperElement, London, 2014
Bandler, Richard, Roberti, Alessio and Fitzpatrick, Owen, *The Ultimate Introduction to NLP: How to Build a Successful Life*, HarperElement, London, 2012
Bandler, Richard and Thompson, Garner, *The Secrets of Being Happy: The Technology of Health, Hope and Harmony*, IM Press, 2011
Colbert, Brian, *The Happiness Habit*, Gill & Macmillan, Dublin, 2009
Colbert, Brian, *From Ordinary to Extraordinary*, Gill & Macmillan, Dublin, 2013
Fitzpatrick, Owen, *Not Enough Hours: The Secret to Making Every Second Count*, Poolbeg Press, Dublin, 2009
Fitzpatrick, Owen, *The Charismatic Edge: The Art of Captivating and Compelling Communication*, Gill & MacMillan, Dublin, 2013
Wilson, Robert Anton, *Prometheus Rising*, New Falcon Publications, Tempe, AZ, 1983
— , *Quantum Psychology*, New Falcon Publications, Tempe, AZ, 1990

DVD AND CD PRODUCTS

Bandler, Richard, *DHE*, CD, 2000

— , *The Art and Science of Nested Loops*, DVD, 2003

— , *Persuasion Engineering*, DVD, 2006

— , *Personal Enhancement Series*, CD, 2010

La Valle, John, *NLP Practitioner Set*, CD, 2009

These and many more DVDs and CDs, both hypnotic and from Richard's seminars, are available from www.nlpstore.com

Bandler, Richard, *Adventures in Neuro-Hypnotic Repatterning*, DVD set and PAL-version videos, 2002

— , *Thirty Years of NLP: How to Live a Happy Life*, DVD set, 2003

These and other products by Richard Bandler are available from Matrix Essential Training Alliance, www.meta-nlp.co.uk; e-mail: enquiries@meta-nlp.co.uk; tel. +44 (0)1749 871126; fax +44 (0)1749 870714

Fitzpatrick, Owen, *Love in Your Life*, Hypnosis CD, 2004

— , *Adventures in Charisma*, DVD set, 2008

— , *Performance Boost*, Hypnosis CD, 2011

— , *Confidence Boost*, Hypnosis CD, 2011

Available from www.nlp.ie.

Fitzpatrick, Owen, et al, *The Online Charisma Training Academy*, Online video & audio, 2013

Available from www.charismatrainingacademy.com

WEBSITES

www.richardbandler.com

www.purenlp.com

www.nlp.ie

www.owenfitzpatrick.com

blog.owenfitzpatrick.com

www.theultimateintroductiontonlp.com

www.charismatrainingacademy.com

www.nlpmovement.com

www.facebook.com/realrichardbandler (Richard's Facebook page)

www.facebook.com/ofi23 (Owen's Facebook page)

www.twitter.com/owenfitzp (Owen's Twitter account)

www.youtube.com/owenjf23 (Owen's YouTube account)

THE SOCIETY OF NEURO-LINGUISTIC PROGRAMMING™

Richard Bandler Licensing Agreement

The Society of Neuro-Linguistic Programming™ is set up for the purpose of exerting quality control over those training programs, services and materials claiming to represent the model of Neuro-Linguistic Programming (NLP). The seal below indicates Society Certification and is usually advertised by Society approved trainers. When you purchase NLP products and seminars, ask to see this seal. This is your guarantee of quality.

It is common experience for many people, when they are introduced to NLP and first begin to learn the technology, to be cautious and concerned with the possible uses and misuses.

As a protection for you and for those around you, the Society of NLP™ now requires participants to sign a licensing agreement which guarantees that those certified in this technology will use it with the highest integrity.

It is also a way to ensure that all the training you attend is of the highest quality and that your trainers are up to date with the constant evolution of the field of Neuro-Linguistic Programming and Design Human Engineering®, etc.

For a list of recommendations, go to:

- http://www.NLPInstitutes.com

- http://www.NLPTrainers.com

The Society of NLP™
NLP Seminars Group International PO Box 424
Hopatcong, NJ 07843, USA
Tel: (973) 770-3600
Website: www.purenlp.com

Copyright 1994–2013 The Society of NLP™ and Richard Bandler